THE GENESIS OF FUTURISM: MARINETTI'S EARLY CAREER AND WRITINGS 1899–1909

BY

GÜNTER BERGHAUS

OCCASIONAL PAPERS
NUMBER 1

PUBLISHED BY
THE SOCIETY FOR ITALIAN STUDIES
1995

PUBLISHED BY

THE SOCIETY FOR ITALIAN STUDIES

THE HONORARY TREASURER
SOCIETY FOR ITALIAN STUDIES
DEPARTMENT OF ITALIAN
THE UNIVERSITY OF LEEDS
LEEDS
LS2 9JT

ISBN 0 9525901 0 7

*The Publication of this volume was made
possible through grants received from the
Italian Cultural Institute and from the
University of Bristol Research Fund*

PRINTED BY
W. S. MANEY & SON LTD
HUDSON ROAD   LEEDS

CONTENTS

INTRODUCTION

F. T. Marinetti, the founder and leader of the Futurist movement, has been the subject of many books and essays. His fundamental rôle in establishing Futurism on the Italian and international art scenes as well as his contribution to modernist literature have been firmly engraved in the chronicles of twentieth-century cultural history. However, his early, pre-Futurist, career has met with little critical attention.

Long before the publication of the *Foundation and Manifesto of Futurism* in 1909, Europe was rife with trends and developments which indicated that a radical change of direction from nineteenth-century culture was afoot. The aim behind my study here is to link the gestation period of Futurism to this general intellectual climate of the period. For this purpose, I shall examine several of the aesthetic and ideological currents with which Marinetti came into contact during his early, pre-Futurist, career, and analyse those elements which influenced his development and served to shape his vision of a new and revolutionary artistic practice.

In the second part I shall then focus on Marinetti's early publications. Three volumes of poetry, three plays, one novella and several journalistic essays will be analysed to show how Marinetti assimilated his sources and how, progressively, he assembled the basic ingredients of the artistic programme which, in 1909, he presented to the world as the *Foundation and Manifesto of Futurism*.

PART ONE

MARINETTI'S PRE-FUTURIST CAREER AND HIS EARLY SOURCES OF INFLUENCE

Life in Egypt and student years: Early literary and political activities

Emilio Angelo Carlo Marinetti, who later called himself Filippo Tommaso,[1] was born, in 1876, in Alexandria in Egypt, as the second son of the Piedmontese lawyer Enrico Marinetti and Amalia Grolli, daughter of a literary professor from Milan.[2] Marinetti senior had come to Egypt with the hope of making his fortune in the European community residing in the country. At that time, Egypt was still part of the Ottoman Empire and came under the rule of the Sultan in Istanbul. The governing authority was the Khedives, viceroys of the Sultan, who had great admiration for the advances of industry and technology in Europe. In the second half of the nineteenth century they embarked on an extensive programme of modernization. As part of this, they had the Suez canal built (finished in 1869), which altered the strategic position of Egypt in the Eastern Mediterranean and greatly enhanced the country's political and economic importance. Investment was sought for a large number of projects, and foreigners were invited to advise on the future development of the region.

---

[1] It seems that the officially registered name in Alexandria and Milan was never used. Marinetti himself gave his full name as Filippo Achille Giulio. His baccalaureate diploma is made out to Philippe Achille Emile, his doctorate diploma to Filippo, his military service card to Emilio. However, his family did not call him by any of these names: to them he was simply Tom.

[2] Marinetti wrote three autobiographical sketches of his early life: 'Autoritratto' in *Scatole d'amore in conserva* (Rome, 1927), pp. 7–28 and partly reprinted in the chapter 'Alessandria d'Egitto' in *Marinetti e il Futurismo* (Rome, 1929), reprinted in *Teoria e invenzione futurista* (in the following quoted as TeI), (Milan, 1969), pp. 503–06; *La grande Milano tradizionale e futurista* and *Una sensibilità italiana nata in Egitto*, both written between 1943 and 1944 and published posthumously by L. de Maria as volume 3 of the *Opere di F. T. Marinetti* (Milan, 1969), (excerpts have been translated in *Marinetti: Selected Writings*, ed. by R. W. Flint [in the following quoted as Flint], (London, 1972)). There are also several autobiographical stories in *Il fascino dell'Egitto* (Milan, 1933). A first 'critical' biography (Tullio Pànteo, *Il poeta Marinetti*) appeared in Milan in 1908 in a popular series of 'Lives of Great Poets'. As Angelo Ragghianti reports in *Marinetteide o Marionetteide* (Rome, 1909), p. 16: 'Tullio Pànteo knew nothing of this publication; his short biographical sketch had been corrected, enlarged, distorted, and had become a volume of 215 pages. He had invoked the intervention of the Law.' The other biographies which appeared during Marinetti's lifetime were no more reliable. After 1945, there appeared an equally subjective work, Walter Vaccari, *Vita e tumulti di F. T. Marinetti* (Milan, 1959). Since Marinetti's wife, and later his daughters, forbade or restricted access to the poet's personal papers, to this day no proper biography that could withstand modern critical standard has seen the light! There is some useful information (and many factual errors) in Donald Marinelli's Ph.D. thesis, *Origins of Theatricality: The Early Life and Career of F. T. Marinetti* (University of Pittsburgh, 1987). An attractive and extremely well-illustrated volume is Claudia Salaris, *Filippo Tommaso Marinetti* (Florence, 1988). The rather novelistic biography by Gino Agnese, *Marinetti: Una vita esplosiva* (Milan, 1990), offers little new information.

FIG. 1.   Marinetti as a schoolboy, aged fourteen

FIG. 2. The young poet Marinetti at the age of eighteen

When Marinetti senior came to Egypt, he found himself in a haven of speculation and economic adventurism. He set up a lawyer's office in Alexandria and conducted civil litigations and court cases, as well as giving advice on financial deals. Compared to cosmopolitan Cairo, Alexandria was still a very oriental city.[3] The amenities of modern life were largely absent, but the life-style of the foreigners, centred around sumptuous residences, was very much to the liking of the Marinettis who, from 1872 to 1894, lived in one of these villas by the sea.

When the two children reached school age, they were sent not to a local Italian school (of which there were several), but to a French institution run by Jesuit priests. The *Collège Saint-François-Xavier* was a school for the foreign élite. It was international in outlook, had an arts-based curriculum, and pursued a solidly Catholic educational programme. Tuition at the school was conducted in French, which became like a second mother-tongue to Filippo Tommaso. Through his mother he was introduced to Italian literature and poetry. As both an expatriate and a woman, Amalia Marinetti was cut off from the social and cultural life around her. The reading of poetry was her main consolation and, as a mother, she endeavoured to acquaint her sons with a comprehensive body of European literature.

From an early age, Marinetti was a prolific writer of poetry. In order to see his works published he founded his own magazine, *Le Papyrus: Revue bi-mensuelle littéraire, artistique, fantaisiste et mondaine*. Twenty-one numbers appeared between February 1894 and January 1895, and they had a remarkably professional touch. Marinetti's own contributions not only comprised of poems, but also essays on literary questions, new artistic trends, and political issues in which he revealed himself as being well-informed about the socialist and anarchist movements. His artistic credo did not find much favour with the French priests at school. In fact, they were aghast when he published in his journal an essay defending Zola and Naturalism against the critics. But it was not only Zola's depiction of French society and, in particular, of the lower strata of society, that interested Marinetti. He was 'obsessed', as he called it, with Zola, the chronicler of the Modern Age, the author of the railway novel *La Bête humaine*.[4] When he chose to support his literary arguments by bringing into class some novels by Zola (at that time regarded as obscene and immoral) he was expelled from the college.

Some time before Marinetti's school education came to a sudden end, his father had been making arrangements to move back to Italy. His three offices in Alessandria, Cairo and Khartoum had afforded him a lucrative career. But the rising tide of Muslim and Egyptian nationalism and the political unrest directed against corruption in the Khedival government made the life of European businessmen ever more precarious. It had become a frequent occurrence to see rioting mobs roaming through the streets of Alessandria, assaulting foreigners, and pillaging their homes. Marinetti senior decided that it was time to enjoy the fruits of

---

[3] A suggestive evocation of the city at this time can be found in E. M. Forster's *Alexandria: A History and a Guide*, and Lawrence Durrell's *Justine*.

[4] See the chapter 'Zola obsessed me' in *Una sensibilità italiana*, p. 218 (Flint 313).

his twenty years of expatriate labour. His son was to study law at an Italian university and then take over his father's practice. At least, this was his plan. He made arrangements to settle in Milan and for Filippo Tommaso to complete his schooling at a *liceo* in Lombardy or Piedmont. But, as it turned out, his son's distinctly French-oriented education meant that it was more appropriate for him to finish his studies at a French *lycée*.

Therefore, in April 1894, young Tommaso was sent to Paris to take his baccalauréat at the Sorbonne. Understandably, the *grisettes* of the Latin Quarter held much more fascination for him than the professors at school, and he spent more time in the cafés than in the lecture halls. He also frequented the cabarets and music halls of Montmartre and gained access to the salons of Parisian literary society, thereby becoming well-informed on the latest trends in French art and literature.

Despite the artistic and hedonistic distractions offered to him in Paris, Filippo Tommaso passed his exams at the first attempt and was awarded the *Diplome de Bachelier de l'Enseignement secondaire classique* on 13 July 1894. Soon afterwards he returned to Italy and, in November 1895, enrolled at the University of Pavia to study law, in accordance with his father's wishes. After a transfer to Genoa he graduated, on 14 July 1899, with a thesis on *The Crown in Parliamentary Government*.

Marinetti's commitment to his legal studies had been very half-hearted. He derived some satisfaction from the political and philosophical aspects of the course, but spent most of his time pursuing his true calling, poetry. His student years were enormously productive for his literary career. He commuted regularly between France and Italy in order to keep in contact with his friends and acquaintances of the Parisian art scene. He found a retreat from university life in a small village near his father's hometown of Voghera. Here, in Godiasco, he wrote most of his verses that were deemed fit for publication in respected literary magazines, such as *La Plume, La nouvelle Revue, Mercure de France, La Vogue, Vers et Prose, Gil Blas*, etc.

Although in his autobiography Marinetti has more to say on his *éducation érotique* than his *études scolaires* or *artistiques*, his notebook of the years 1895–98 shows that he took an interest in

> a variety of topics, including Symbolist poetry, Pre-Raphaelite art, and Japanese painting. It is the work of a youthful and inquisitive intellectual who seems, from the extent of his quotations, to be particularly impressed by the Symbolist poet Henri de Régnier.[5]

Symbolism, inaugurated in 1886 with the publication of Jean Moréas's manifesto in *Le Figaro*, was the most influential school of literature in the 1890s, and Marinetti converted whole-heartedly to its aesthetics. After his first stay in Paris his style of poetry underwent a dramatic change and, over the next ten years, he became a recognized and respected member of the Symbolist school.

---

[5] *F. T. Marinetti and Futurism: Catalogue of an Exhibition in the Beinecke Rare Book and Manuscript Library* (Yale University, 1983), no. 2.

One of the movement's most prominent leaders was Gustave Kahn. He had taken notice of Marinetti's literary production and, in 1898, awarded him the first prize in a national poetry competition which he had organized together with Catulle Mendès. The award-winning poem was publicly recited by Sarah Bernhardt, and Gustave Kahn became Marinetti's mentor.[6] His *vers libres* style was a major influence on Marinetti's Symbolist as well as early Futurist poetry.[7] Kahn introduced his young disciple to the French cultural élite, to newspaper editors and publishers, actors, playwrights and theatre directors. Within a few years, Marinetti was established as a major new talent on the French literary scene.

Marinetti also served as a kind of literary agent, getting young French poets published in Italy and placing recent Italian writing in French magazines and anthologies. His name appeared as collaborator on a number of literary journals, and from 1898 he functioned as *secrétaire général* of *Anthologie-Revue de France et d'Italie: Récueil mensuel de littérature et d'art*, a poetry magazine founded in 1897 by Edward Sansot-Orland and dedicated to popularizing French Symbolism in Italy and making the Italian Symbolist poets known in France.

As a result of his activities as a 'literary manager', Marinetti became a major force on the Italian literary scene. In 1899, he published an *Anthologie des poètes italiens contemporains*. His own views on contemporary Italian poetry were voiced in an essay, 'Le mouvement poétique en Italie', printed in the April 1899 issue of *La Vogue*.[8] His assessment of the majority of Italian poets was devastatingly negative: 'What is the state of mind of the Italian poets? They live in solitude in small, dead cities in the manner of melancholic kings left behind in their sunken capitals.'[9] He regarded them as materialists and positivists, who vegetated in a climate of spiritual indifference and were totally insensitive to the cultural crisis of the time. There were, of course, exceptions, such as Carducci, Pascoli, and d'Annunzio, who were the inspiration for a new generation of poets represented in his anthology by, amongst others, Butti, Boito, Corradini, Lucini, Marradi, Moschino, Negri, Panzacchi, Pastonchi, Roccatagliata Ceccardi, and Térésah. But the majority of Italian poets Marinetti saw as being steeped in academism and hemmed in by their adherence to classical verse structures.

In another essay, 'Les jeunes romanciers italiens', published in the December 1899 issue of *La Vogue*, he offered his assessment of the contemporary Italian novel and some interesting thoughts on why French decadent literature had to serve as a model for new writing in Italy. A key aspect of this was language. Since there was no Italian equivalent of the poetic experiments undertaken by the French Symbolists on a phonetic and syntactical level, Marinetti — as well as other Italian

---

[6] In *Una sensibilità italiana*, p. 243 (Flint 329) he refers to him as his 'patrono'.

[7] On Kahn and his prominent rôle in the development of Free Verse poetry see Clive Scott, *Vers Libre: The Emergence of Free Verse in France 1886–1914* (Oxford, 1990).

[8] The essay was an early manifesto of his aesthetic convictions, which he kept up with slight alteration for nearly ten years, as the republication of the essay under the title 'La poésie italienne contemporaine' in *La Rénovation estétique* (January 1908) testifies.

[9] 'Le mouvement poétique en Italie', p. 61.

writers of the period[10] — had to look towards French models when they endeavoured to find a new idiom to communicate their poetic concerns. As he said in an
essay of 1901: 'The classic line, the equilibrium, the temperateness have disappeared from art, just as order, meditation and silence have disappeared from
life.'[11] But not so in Italy. For this reason Marinetti chose to follow the example set
by French decadent literature, which for him possessed 'a style, where the unity of
the book disintegrates in order to open up the freedom of the page; where the unity
of the page desintegrates to give space to the freedom of the sentence; where the
unity of the sentence disintegrates to give room to the freedom of the word [*liberté
du mot*].'[12] From there it was only a matter of a few small steps to arrive at the
Futurist *mots en liberté (parole in libertà)*. In the late-nineteenth century, however,
the conditions for this were not yet fully developed. As Marinetti rightly observed:
'Italian poetry has changed very little since Leopardi. To the eye of the observer it
appears most unsophisticated, absolutely unaffected by the modern spirit and
contemptuous of the heaving research that animates the soul of our century.'[13] This
lack of a 'modern spirit' was a cultural as well as socio-economic fact. The Italian
bourgeoisie was overwhelmingly conservative in their political and social attitudes
and rejected French decadent culture from a moral, as well as artistic, viewpoint.
Therefore, Marinetti saw himself forced into an increasingly oppositional rôle
against 'this lugubrious *fin-de-siècle*' and sought to 'kill our antiquated heart'.[14] He
cultivated the image of a rebel and anarchical hero who sympathized with the
political revolutionaries of his age and expressed their *beaux gestes libertaires* in his
own iconoclastic poetry.

As these essays of 1899–1901 make clear, it was not only the specific conditions
of Marinetti's education in Alexandria (or, even worse, a certain cultural snobbery
common amongst the Italian élite) that propelled Marinetti to write his early works
in the French language. He had good reason to regard the expressive range of the
Italian language as inadequate at present for communicating the concerns of the
modern age, and therefore continued to write his poetry in French rather than
Italian.

Marinetti made a great impact with his first collection, *La Conquête des étoiles*,
published in 1902. Reviews appeared in *Le Figaro, Le Mercure de France,
L'Hermitage, La nouvelle Revue, Gil Blas, Critique internationale* and a large
number of Italian newspapers. After this resounding success, Marinetti's father
accepted the fact that his son was never going to become a practising lawyer. The
strained relationship between the two healed and when, in 1902, Amalia Marinetti
died, Filippo Tommaso moved his residence to Via Senato 2 and shared the large
flat with his father until the latter's death in 1907. He published more poems, prose,

---

[10] See Guy Tosi, 'Aperçu sur les influences littéraires françaises en Italie dans le dernier tiers du XIX
siècle', in *Rivista di letterature moderne e comparate*, 19 (1966), 165–70.
[11] F. T. Marinetti, 'Mascagni contre Wagner', in *La Plume*, no. 283 (15 February 1901), p. 128.
[12] Ibid, p. 127.
[13] 'Le Mouvement poétique en Italie', p. 61.
[14] F. T. Marinetti, 'Vittorio Pica', in *Anthologie-Revue*, 2, no. 7 (May 1899), p. 131.

and dramatic works; entered into the literary debates of the time with his polemical essays; and began to exercise considerable control and influence through his editorial activities.

His personal papers of these years, now preserved at Yale University, reveal his insatiable appetite for politics, philosophy and poetry. These writings include descriptive notes on government and democracy in France, an article about Florence, essays on Mallarmé. He also compiled literature on Rachilde (the playwright whose work helped launch Paul Fort's Théâtre d'Art), and Maurice Barrès (one of the first Parisian editors and poets to hail and credit Baudelaire with the new perspective on poetry that was to become Symbolism). There are also writings in which Marinetti attempts to understand the aims of socialism.[15]

Marinetti's student years were not only important for his career as a poet and literary manager, but also because they enabled him to gain ground on the ideological front. The compulsory reading for his legal and political studies at university was complemented by his interest in left-wing politics and contemporary philosophy. Marinetti's *Weltanschauung* during this period was a mixture of beliefs derived from a large number of different sources. He was an admirer of Nietzsche's radical individualism and Bergson's dynamic concept of the universe, but he also studied Marx and Engels, Bakunin and Sorel.

Two of his closest friends at that time were the anarchist poets Gian Pietro Lucini and Umberto Notari, with whom he frequented various libertarian circles in Lombardy. Although the Italian anarchists had left the PSI in 1891 and had founded their own Anarchist-Socialist Revolutionary Party, their main range of influence was exercised via the syndicalist movement.[16] Many artists and writers with a 'revolutionary' mentality were active in these circles. Marinetti was one of them, and he continued to declaim his poetry in their meeting halls and give lectures on art and politics right up until the mid-1910s.[17] The libertarian societies were an important recruiting ground for Marinetti, the enterprising literary manager. Not only poets such as Roccatagliata Ceccardi, Buzzi, Cavacchioli, Jannelli, and Tommei, but also the painters Carrà, Boccioni, Russolo, and Balla were supporters of the anarchist movement and contributed to its journals and magazines.[18] The iconoclastic mentality of the artists Marinetti gathered around himself soon found a reflection in his own writing. Fanette Roche-Pézard even goes as far as to suggest that Marinetti's early poetry was influenced by the style and tone of anarchist magazines, brochures, and posters.[19]

---

[15] Marinelli, *Origins of Futurist Theatricality*, pp. 72–73.

[16] On Italian anarchism see Pier Carlo Masini, *Storia degli anarchici italiani da Bakunin a Malatesta, 1862–1892*, Milan 1969, Enzo Santarelli, *Il socialismo anarchico in Italia*, 2nd edn (Milan, 1973); Pier Carlo Masini, *Storia degli anarchici nell'epoca degli attentati* (Milan, 1981).

[17] See Giovanni Lista, 'Marinetti et les anarcho-syndicalistes', in *Présence de F. T. Marinetti*, ed. by J.-C. Marcadé (Lausanne, 1982), pp. 67–85 and Umberto Carpi, *L'estrema avanguardia del Novecento* (Rome, 1985).

[18] See Alberto Ciampi, *Futuristi e anarchici: Quali rapporti?* (Pistoia, 1989).

[19] See her essay 'Marinetti et l'anarchie', in Marcadé, *Présence de F. T. Marinetti*, pp. 127–33.

Unfortunately, there is little concrete information available on Marinetti's political activities as a young student and poet. During the Milan uprising of May 1898 he took great interest in the revolutionary actions on the barricades.[20] He visited meetings held by the Socialist Party and the trade unions; he listened to speeches held by Arturo Labriola; he made the acquaintance of the socialist leaders Turati and Kuliscioff, and he became friends with the Revolutionary Syndicalist Walter Mocchi.[21] Mocchi was, together with Enrico Leone and Arturo Labriola, a prominent syndicalist of Sorelian conviction and co-editor of *L'avanguardia socialista*. Marinetti must have got to know Mocchi, who was married to the famous opera singer Emma Carelli, through his activities as a reviewer of Milanese opera productions[22] (see below, pp. 41–43). Together, they attended Verdi's funeral in 1901, and were actively involved in the General Strike of September 1904 which Giolitti characterized as 'the dress rehearsal of the revolution'.[23] Mocchi is mentioned again in conjunction with the General Elections of 1909 and the *First Futurist Political Manifesto*.[24] Marinetti's anarcho-syndicalist leanings came to the fore again when, in the same year, he took to the streets with the Milanese students to demonstrate against the death sentence passed on the Catalan anarchist and educationalist Francesco Ferrer for his supposed rôle in the violence during the Barcelona General Strike of 26–29 July 1909.[25]

Some information on Marinetti's political thinking during this early period can be gleaned from two essays of 1900 and 1901. 'Les Emeutes milanaises de mai 1898' reveals his interest in the social problems of the underdeveloped, southern parts of Italy and the deeper causes of the unrest that shook Milan in 1898. He expresses his sympathies with the socialists on the barricades and shows a profound disgust at the carnage caused by General Bava Beccaris. He offers a positive portrait of Turati and Kuliscioff and emphasizes that the revolt was not fanned by the Socialist Party. Rather than promoting open violence, they fought with legal, parliamentarian means because they knew 'how dangerous and useless it is for the future of collectivism to unleash a partial revolution in Italy. As a matter

[20] See his essay 'Les Emeutes milanaises de mai 1898: Paysages et silhouettes', in *La Revue blanche*, 22, no. 173 (15 August 1900), 561–70 and the poem, 'La mendiante d'au-delà', in *Anthologie-Revue*, 1, no. 9 (June 1898), p. 175 [in *Scritti francesi* p. 21].

[21] See *La grande Milano*, pp. 19–20, 26–30. On Mocchi's biography see Franco Andreucci & Tommaso Detti, *Il movimento operaio italiano: Dizionario biografico 1853–1943*, 3 (Rome, 1977), 484–89.

[22] Mocchi gave up his political career in 1906 to dedicate himself fully to the management of his wife's brilliant operatic career. Carelli later became the director of La Scala in Milan and Mocchi a theatrical entrepreneur. Both were of invaluable help to Marinetti when later, during his Futurist years, he required access to large theatres for his *serate*.

[23] See Nino Valeri, *La lotta politica in Italia dall'Unità al 1925* (Florence, 1966), p. 283. Mocchi was, in fact, one of the key organizers of the event.

[24] See *La grande Milano*, pp. 19, 27, 28.

[25] See *La grande Milano*, p. 81. The tragic event of Ferrer's execution and the international protest it caused has been described in Emma Goldman, 'Francesco Ferrer: The Modern School', in E. Goldman, *Anarchism and Other Essays* (New York, 1911) and Joan Connelly Ullman, *The Tragic Week* (Cambridge, Massachusetts, 1968).

of fact, no country in the world shows itself less prepared for social reform by way of revolutionary change than Italy.'[26] The largest part of the essay contains an evocative description of the street fighting in Milan. Marinetti visited the barricades erected in the city centre, only to find himself in the midst of several skirmishes. He had every reason to fear for his life and decided 'to avoid the mishap of being hit by a bullet. So I went home and observed the drama from the height of my balcony.'[27] His observations both from safe distance and close quarters were complemented by reflections on the pre-rational motives behind the revolt. Marinetti was reluctant to accept that only socio-economic factors caused the populace to rebel. He had witnessed how the rage of the common people erupted in a spontaneous, convulsive form and felt compelled to apply his study of Bergson and Sorel (see below, pp. 17–20, 22–27) to this example of a voluntary, intuitive rebellion: 'In my view, one has to look elsewhere for the origin of the riots of 6 May, such as psychological forces both deeply rooted and complex. [...] Apart from the famine, the impressive events need to be explained by [the people's] horizon, the climate, and atavistic behaviour.'

The general thrust of this essay shows Marinetti to be a humanitarian thinker concerned with the living conditions of the masses, rather than as a revolutionary socialist or anarchist. The same can be said about the other political essay of this period, published on the occasion of the opening of the first Popular University in Milan.[28] The institution bore close resemblance to the *bourses du travail* in France and *Arbeiterschulen* in Germany and, later on, became a meeting place of Revolutionary Syndicalists, anarchists and socialists, where Marinetti himself gave many lectures and poetry readings.[29] The essay reported on the inauguration ceremony of this progressive educational organisation, where d'Annunzio read from his poem *La Chanson de Garibaldi*. The event appeared to Marinetti to be a good omen, for it showed that the University was not going to be concerned with teaching grammar and spelling, but 'the principles of intelligence'. This kind of teaching would enable the workers to argue, reason, and work with their brains — a necessary precondition for shaping society and understanding how it functions. But d'Annunzio's presence augurs yet more: if workers begin to learn from such eminent spiritual leaders, they will widen their cultural horizon and contribute to more than just the material well-being of society. It was an exciting experience for Marinetti to see 4,000 workers at the Teatro Olympia listening to d'Annunzio's verses and to appreciate the difference 'to the violent simplicity of Turati's speeches or Ferri's bludgeon strokes and oratory style as colourless as a white loaf of bread.' This fact

---

[26] 'Les Emeutes milanaises de mai 1898', p. 575.
[27] Ibid., p. 571.
[28] 'L'Université populaire de Milan et G. d'Annunzio', in *La Revue blanche* (15 March 1901), pp. 458–59.
[29] See the chapter 'Futurist Politics in 1910–15 and Their Influence on the Radical Left' in my forthcoming study on *Futurism and Politics* (Oxford, 1995).

alone offered to Marinetti 'a marvellous foreboding of the intellectual and moral renaissance of Italy'.[30]

Dr Marinetti (this is how he signed most of his essays of this period) was, so it seems, far more serious in his political engagement than most members of the late Lombard *scapigliatura*.[31] But his decision to become a poet rather than a lawyer meant that his contribution to the development of a new Italian society came through the medium of books rather than through an involvement on a party-political or administrative level. He himself admitted that he remained 'an observer',[32] especially of 'the psychology of the masses'[33] and of the charismatic leaders of the period. It seems that Marinetti was attracted to all those movements that could be called 'revolutionary', whatever their colours might be. His main sympathies lay with the anarchists and Revolutionary Syndicalists, but he was also an ardent nationalist and an admirer of Crispi, whom he proclaimed as his 'preferred great Italian patriot'.[34] He was therefore unwilling to lend his support to Labriola, and even less so to the Socialist leaders, Turati and Ferri. As he himself said: 'My passion for Italy forbids me to savour any internationalisms.'[35] As Marinetti's autobiographical and critical writings testify, he was an engaged witness to the revolutionary upheavals of his time, but he did not adhere to any one political camp. Despite his interest in politics, he did not become a political activist, nor, in fact, a *poète engagé*. However, his literary production was strongly informed by the philosophical and political trends of his time. Once these had been assimilated and developed into a personal *Weltanschauung*, they could serve as a foundation on which to build a new and original system of thought — Futurism.

French philosophy in the late nineteenth century: The influence of Nietzsche and Bergson

French philosophical thinking in the second half of the nineteenth century had moved from a late-positivist phase to a far more idealist, spiritualist position,

---

[30] 'De merveilleux présages pour la renaissance intellectuelle et morale de l'Italie' is his exact wording, predating his concept of an Italian cultural revolution which he was to outline in the chapter 'Il proletariato dei geniali' in *Democrazia futurista* (TeI 350–54) and in *Al di là del comunismo* (TeI 409–24). For a detailed analysis of these writings see my book on *Futurism and Politics*.

[31] Although the high-period of these bohemian littérateurs was the 1860s and 70s, their social-critical attitudes prevailed until the turn of the century and mixed well with the more recent trend of French Symbolism. See Gaetano Mariani, *Storia della scapigliatura* (Caltanissetta, 1967).

[32] *La grande Milano*, p. 28.

[33] The term 'la psychologie des foules' is used in 'Les Emeutes milanaises de mai 1898'. One must assume that Marinetti at that time was already familiar with the writings of Le Bon, Durkheim, Tarde and Adam on the topic.

[34] *La grande Milano*, p. 18.

[35] *La grande Milano*, p. 28. Such an uneasy mixture between anarchism and nationalism was not uncommon in the syndicalist movement (see David D. Roberts, *The Syndicalist Tradition and Italian Fascism* (Manchester, 1979)). Later on, even militant anarchists such as Dinale, Rygier, de Ambris or Corridoni came out in support of Italian intervention in the First World War. Marinetti's conception of *guerra sola igiene del mondo* was quite widely discussed in anarchist circles (see Carpi, *L'estrema avanguardia*, pp. 15–53) and did not differ much from the views expressed in *La guerra sociale: Settimanale anarchico interventista*.

inspired particularly by the teachings of Maine de Biron. The growth of psychology as a new 'science' led to an examination of the conditions under which the mind operates and to a new approach in the study of sensation and perception. We can observe a transition from the investigation into *the world* to an examination of *my world*, including the rôle of emotions and volition in the process of philosophical enquiry.

This new generation of thinkers refused to limit philosophy to the analysis of material phenomena. Human consciousness and understanding of the world were no longer explained in terms of externally caused sensations. Man was seen not only as a sensing being, but as endowed with a personality that controlled the efforts of the will. The term 'spiritualism' is often employed to characterize this new philosophical trend, meaning that the rejection of materialism and empiricism went hand in hand with the assertion of the ontological priority of spirit to matter. As a corollary, it carried with it an emphasis on the rôle of intuition, spontaneity, voluntary effort, and subconscious vision.

Many idealist and transcendental philosophies held sway in France in the latter part of the nineteenth century. The phenomenal world was declared an appearance of something else which is inaccessible to us through the methods of positivist science. Drawing heavily on Neo-Kantian metaphysics, the question of the intelligibility of reality again became the centre of attention. In this conflict between 'interiority' and 'exteriority', science was forced into a framework of idealist thought. The whole apparatus of reflective consciousness was re-examined, leading to highly speculative results that could be admired for their imaginative and poetic quality, but could not always qualify to be considered as a 'serious' philosophy.

None the less, or rather as a consequence of this, these writings often exercised considerable influence in the world of letters. Marinetti gave evidence in his early writings of having been under the influence of these thinkers. One of the most influential and popular philosophers of the period was Friedrich Nietzsche, and there can be little doubt that Marinetti absorbed some of his key concepts from an early stage. There are many references to Nietzschean ideas in his early poetry, and his play *Le Roi Bombance* reveals an intimate knowledge of *Thus Spake Zarathustra*.

It was probably in Paris that Marinetti began to imbibe Nietzschean thought, either indirectly or through reading the first translations that began to appear in France from 1893 onwards. But, it is equally possible that he familiarized himself with the German philosopher during his student years in Italy, where the French translations edited by the Societé du Mercure de France[36] were widely read and discussed in literary and intellectual circles. With the appearance of the first Italian translations of Nietzsche's works,[37] the general public began to indulge in a

[36] By 1905, nearly all his major writings were available in the French edition of the *Œuvres complètes de Frédéric Nietzsche*.

[37] The series of Italian translations began in 1898 with *Jenseits von Gut und Böse*, followed in 1899 by *Also sprach Zarathustra*. Both works quickly ran through several editions and were soon supplemented by *Die fröhliche Wissenschaft* (1901), *Geburt der Tragödie* (1907) and *Ecce Homo* (1910).

Nietzsche cult. A large number of essays in cultural magazines and literary journals testifies to the increasing popularity of the German philosopher.[38] M. A. Stefani summarized the early reception of Nietzsche in Italy:

> At the end of the nineteenth and the beginning of the twentieth century, Nietzsche was in the first instance a curiosity item. He was regarded as an intellectual who had said some 'strange things' in a language so ultra-modern as to give us a taste of the things to come. He was hardly understood at the time. For European and, even more so, Italian culture, Nietzsche was still a part of the future. He was a phenomenon outside the norm, beyond his time, an anticipator of a new epoch [...] Then, in the years preceding the First World War, Nietzschean thinking rapidly disseminated in Italy, although only the superficial aspects of it, such as the doctrine of the *Übermensch* and the *Wille zur Macht*, were cultivated.[39]

Probably the most important person to effect this popularization of Nietzsche in Italy was d'Annunzio. Through his essays and literary works a pseudo-Nietzschean Superhero cult gained currency in Italy and conditioned an extremely selective and simplified reception of Nietzsche's philosophy. As Gaia Michelini judged:

> Through d'Annunzio and the various artistic and literary avant-garde circles Nietzsche made his first appearance in the conversations of the world of fashionable salons and official academic culture. [...] It was in the first instance d'Annunzio's picture of Nietzsche, that is: Nietzsche filtered through the provincial and decadent aestheticism and morbid sensuality of the Italian poet, which was destined to have major success and diffusion in Italy, mainly because this was easier to understand, less profound and informed, — and therefore in contradiction to the original. [...] In the early years of the 20th century, everybody was reading Nietzsche. He was a philosopher *à la mode*.[40]

It appears that Marinetti, at least initially, sailed on the same wind and shared the general misconceptions about the German philosopher. He drew heavily on the two key concepts that gained general currency at the turn-of-the-century, *der Wille*

---

[38] Between 1892 and 1916, a constantly increasing number of articles was published in *Leonardo, La critica, Il regno, Marzocco* and various other periodicals, followed by the books of Ettore Zoccoli, *Federico Nietzsche* (Turin, 1898 and 1901); Ugo Ruberti, *Leggendo e annotando Federico Nietzsche: Così parlò Zarathustra* (Mantua, 1902); Francesco Orestano, *Le idee fondamentali di Nietzsche nel loro progressivo svolgimento* (Palermo, 1903, 2nd edn 1904); Lucifero Darchini, *Federico Nietzsche e la sua filosofia* (Milan, 1904); Giacomo Molle, *La concezione materialistica del diritto nella filosofia di Nietzsche* (Oneglia, 1905); Edmondo Sacerdotti, *Federico Nietzsche* (Bagni di Chianciano, 1905), Tito Tosi, *F. Nietzsche, R. Wagner e la tragedia greca* (Florence, 1905), etc. See Manuela Angela Stefani, *Nietzsche in Italia: Rassegna bibliografica, 1893–1970* (Assisi, 1975).

[39] Stefani, *Nietzsche in Italia*, pp. 7–8.

[40] Gaia Michelini, *Nietzsche nell'Italia di d'Annunzio* (Palermo, 1978), pp. 13 and 18. On d'Annunzio's *superuomismo* see Guy Tosi, 'D'Annunzio découvre Nietzsche (1892–1894)', in *Italianistica*, no. 3 (1973), 481–513; Francesco Piga, *Il mito del superuomo in Nietzsche e d'Annunzio* (Florence, 1979); Vittorio Vettori, *Gabriele d'Annunzio e il mito del Superuomo* (Rome, 1981).

zur Macht[41] and *der Übermensch*,[42] and interpreted them along the same line as most of his compatriots.

The concept of the 'Will to Power' has a rather chequered history in the development of Nietzsche's philosophy. In the early writings, he regarded political power, like wordly success, as a corrupting influence and therefore presented them as 'evil'.[43] However, his acknowledgement of the Will to Power as a basic psychological instinct led him to reconsider its dynamic potential for human development. His study of Greek civilization and the rôle of the *agon* principle within it suggested the possibility that the Will to Power could be envisaged as a means to excel and to surpass others in the enterprise of generating cultural values out of Nature. The Will to Power was therefore not corrupting *per se*; if pursued by a noble mind, it could indeed be regarded as beneficial to mankind.

In the aphorism, *Striving For Excellence*,[44] Nietzsche devises a scale of power: at the bottom is primitive man, who directs his aggressions against others and rules with brawn and sword. Only barbarians strive for power and impose their tyrannical will on others.[45] At the top of the ladder is the ascetic, who has himself under complete control and therefore achieves the highest position of excellence. He has overcome the normal breed of humans through sheer mental will power. Everyone is in awe and admiration of him and cedes him the rôle of guide and counsel of the people. A complete picture of this scale from bottom to top, Nietzsche argues, would equal 'a history of culture': at the lower level of civilization, power is a 'demon',[46] whilst 'true power', as exercised by artists, philosophers and saints, is a force of reason and morality and therefore beneficial to

---

[41] A detailed account of how Nietzsche developed and revised the concept is given by Walter Kaufmann, *Nietzsche: Philosopher, Psychologist, Antichrist*, 4th edn (Princeton, New Jersey, 1974), pp. 178–207. See also his chapter on the 'Nietzsche Legend' and the posthumous falsification of the idea. For a critique of Kaufmann's interpretation see Gerd-Günther Grau, *Ideologie und Wille zur Macht: Zeitgemäe Betrachtungen über Nietzsche* (Berlin, 1984). Other recent positions on the problem include R. J. Hollingdale, *Nietzsche* (London, 1973); Wolfgang Müller-Lauter, *Nietzsches Lehre vom Willen zur Macht*, in *Nietzsche Studien*, 3 (1974), 1–60; Willard Mittelmann, 'The Relation Between Nietzsche's Theory of the Will to Power and His Earlier Conception of Power', in *Nietzsche-Studien*, 9 (1980), 122–41; Maudemarie Clark, 'Nietzsche's Doctrines of the Will to Power', in *Nietzsche-Studien*, 12 (1983), 458–68.

[42] The widespread and heterogeneous use of the concept has been analysed in *Der Übermensch: Eine Diskussion*, ed. by Ernst Benz (Zurich, 1961). I am using the German term here, because none of the English translations, Superman, Overman, etc., carry the range of associations that are present in the German word and, in fact, very much distort the meaning behind Nietzsche's conception. A useful clarification of the term and its derivation is offered in Walter Kaufmann, *Nietzsche: Philosopher, Psychologist, Antichrist*, 4th edn (1974), pp. 307–16. See also my discussion below, pp. 65–71.

[43] For the Nietzsche quotations I follow the common practice to refer to his published writings by title, book, section, which facilitates the use of any of the many Nietzsche editions in any language. When referring to the posthumous publications, I use the *Kritische Gesamtausgabe der Werke* (KGW), ed. by G. Colli and M. Montinari. In this instance, see *Untimely Meditations*, IV, 11 and *Der griechische Staat*, KGW III.2, 262.

[44] *Dawn*, p. 113.

[45] See KGW v, 582 (Manuscript 6, fragment 206): 'The desire to rule has often appeared to me as a sign of inward weakness: they fear their own slave soul and shroud it in a royal cloak.'

[46] See *Dawn*, p. 262.

FIG. 3. Marinetti in his flat in Milan, Via Senato 2

mankind. Philosophy especially, as 'the most spiritual Will to Power',[47] enables us 'to raise our eyes above the horizon of the animal [. . .] and to push towards man as something that stands high above us.'[48]

In *Thus Spake Zarathustra*, Nietzsche argues against Darwin's principle of Struggle for Existence and contends that man does not strive to preserve his existence, but to enhance himself. The Will to Power is not a will to assert oneself over others, but to achieve self-realization.[49] In order to reach this aim, humans have to overcome their dependency on the instinctual drives and to 'organize the chaos within themselves'.[50] The dualistic concept of the Dionysian/Apollonian nature of mankind is repudiated in Nietzsche's later writings in favour of a monistic substance with various (mental and physical) accidentals, all of which may change with historical circumstances. It is not a question of Nature *versus* Culture, flesh *versus* spirit, but rather 'spirit is the life that itself cuts into life'.[51] The spiritual life is not opposed to physical existence, but enhances it and lifts it onto a different level of self-fulfilment. Culture, when it is no longer a mere 'decoration of life, [. . .but] a new and improved *physis*',[52] becomes a 'power' that changes life and sublates the dichotomy of culture and nature (or art and life, as Marinetti is later to call it).

[47] *Beyond Good and Evil*, p. 9.
[48] *Untimely Meditations*, III, 5.
[49] *Zarathustra*, II, 12 (On Overcoming Oneself). See also his arguments against 'the scholarly oxens who have suspected me of Darwinism' in *Ecce Homo*, III, 1.
[50] *Untimely Meditations*, II, 10.
[51] *Zarathustra*, II, 8 (Of Famous Philosophers).
[52] *Untimely Meditations*, II, 10.

The discovery of the monistic principle of the Will to Power enabled Nietzsche to establish a new concept of human psychology. What he called 'overcoming' (Überwindung) anticipated Freud's concept of 'sublimation'.[53] In Nietzsche's mature writings, the most powerful man is the one who is master over his impulses and can control his passions, not in order to repress them, but to lift them onto a higher plane. This 'sublimation work' is a creative process that gives form to what otherwise only exists in us as unconscious potential. The Will to Power integrates man's impulses into the sublime totality of his nature and helps him fulfil his human potential.

Man who has risen to this state of complete self-realization is *superior* to humans in their natural state and can therefore be called *Super*-man. It is man who has overcome himself and has reached the top end of the ladder of fulfilment, where finally he has found his 'true self' ('which does not lie deeply concealed within you, but immeasurably high above you'[54]). The *Übermensch* is the product of *Überwindung*, of overcoming his base material and spiritual condition. Although the human species has developed beyond the natural state of pure beasts, it has to reach higher, to the ideal world of the *Übermensch*, in order to attain its full potential. Hence the image, in *Zarathustra*, of 'man as a rope tied between beast and overman'.[55] The *Übermensch* is not a Superman in the modern sense of the word. Nietzsche repeatedly defends himself against the suspicion of hero-worship and insists that the *Übermensch* is an '"idealistic" type of a higher kind of man, half "saint" and half "genius"'.[56] He has 'surveyed everything his nature presents in strength and weakness and then moulds it into an artistic plan until everything appears as art and reason.'[57] He is a man of 'highest accomplishment',[58] 'a spirit who has become free',[59] who has fulfilled the 'totality' of his human nature by 'overcoming all resistance' and 'disciplining himself to perfection'.[60]

---

[53] He also uses the terms *aufheben* (sublate) and *vergeistigen* (spiritualize). When he employs the word *sublimieren* (like, for example, in *Human, All-too Human*, 1) it has the older meaning as employed in chemistry. However, there is a distinctly Freudian concept behind Aphorism 95 of *Assorted Opinions and Maxims* in the second volume of *Human, All-too Human*, where he speaks of Christianity as the result of 'sublimierte Geschlechtlichkeit' (sublimated sexuality). The meaning here is, of course, entirely negative, whilst the notion of art, culture and philosophy as a sublimated Will to Power is a positive concept. On Nietzsche's importance as a psychologist see Ludwig Klages, *Die psychologischen Errungenschaften Nietzsches*, 4th edn (Bonn, 1979); Friedrich Tramer, 'Friedrich Nietzsche und Sigmund Freud', in *Jahrbuch für Psychologie und Psychotherapie*, 7 (1960), 325–50; Henri F. Ellenberger, *The Discovery of the Unconscious* (London, 1970), pp. 271–78; Richard Waugaman, 'The Intellectual Relationship between Nietzsche and Freud', in *Psychiatry*, 36 (1973), 458–67; Rollo May, 'Nietzsches Beitrag zur Psychologie' in *Symposium*, 28 (1974), 58–73; Walter Kaufmann, 'Nietzsche als der erste große Psychologe', in *Nietzsche-Studien*, 7 (1978), 261–87.

[54] *Untimely Meditations*, III, 1.

[55] *Zarathustra*, Prologue, § 4.

[56] *Ecce Homo*, III, 1.

[57] *Gay Science*, p. 290.

[58] Ibid.

[59] *Twighlight of Gods*, IX, 38.

[60] *Twighlight*, IX, 49.

In the popular reception of Nietzsche's philosophy many of these finer points were commonly overlooked. The simplified and therefore misleading interpretations of the concepts of the Will To Power and of the Superman also affected Marinetti's understanding of the German philosopher. As we shall see in the next chapter, his early poems and plays testified to this distorted assimilation of Nietzschean thought at the turn of the century.

Another philosopher whom Marinetti acknowledged as having had a major influence on him was Henri Bergson.[61] In the *Supplement to the Manifesto of Futurist Literature* of 1912 he says that critics have assumed that his anti-intellectual attitudes are a reflection of his familiarity with the writings of Bergson. He asserts that already in 1902, when publishing *La Conquête des étoiles*, he possessed such a conviction. He then goes on to explain the rôle of intellect and intuition in poetic creation and uses the same criteria as Bergson. Flora, in his study *From Romanticism to Futurism*, identifies a large number of further agreements between Bergson's and Marinetti's theories, most importantly the concepts of the *élan vital*, voluntarism and intuition, of time and duration and, derived from this, of simultaneity and interpenetration.

Bergson's exposition of these categories can be found in *Essai sur les données immédiates de la conscience* (1889) and *Matière et mémoire: Essais sur la relation du corps à l'esprit* (1896).[62] In these works, he offered an alternative to the mechanistic tendency in positivist philosophy and the determinist and rationalist thinking of his time. His philosophy exemplified, as Bertrand Russell termed it, a 'revolt against reason'[63] and was concerned with purifying science from 'scientism', which Bergson regarded as metaphysics masquerading as scientific knowledge.

In Bergson's writings, different objects of investigation are assigned to science and metaphysics. While the intellect of the scientist is concerned with a rational analysis of physical objects, the metaphysician seeks to arrive at an intuitive or immediate understanding of the spiritual world. The intellect is only able to reflect on inert matter and mechanical processes, on the structure of discontinuous and immobile bodies. When our intellect applies itself to reality, it cuts out fragments from the Whole, separates them in space and dissects them in time, representing

---

[61] In 1915 he quotes Bergson's anti-rational theories and says, 'We believe with Bergson...' (*crediamo con Bergson...*) TeI 285.

[62] Translated into English as *Time and Free Will* (London, 1910), and *Matter and Memory* (London, 1911). Marinetti will also have read, at a later stage, Bergson's third major work, *L'Evolution créatrice* (1907). For a short and useful introduction to Bergson's philosophy see Gilles Deleuze, *Le Bergsonisme* (Paris, 1966). A more comprehensive account is Vladimir Jankélévitch, *Henri Bergson*, 2nd rev. edn (Paris, 1975). For a recent English assessment see Leszek Kolakowski, *Bergson* (Oxford, 1985) and A. R. Lacey, *Bergson* (London, 1989). For Bergson's influence on literature and the arts see Romeo Arbour, *Henri Bergson et les lettres françaises* (Paris, 1955) and Anthony Edward Pilkington, *Bergson and His Influence: A Reassessment* (Oxford, 1976). A comprehensive analysis of Bergson and Futurism has been promised in the forthcoming book by Mark Antliff, *Inventing Bergson: Cultural Politics and the Parisian Avant-Garde*.

[63] *History of Western Philosophy* (London, 1961), p. 761. A more extensive critique is contained in his *The Philosophy of Henri Bergson* (Cambridge, 1914).

Becoming as a series of states. But this method is insufficient for comprehending the specificity of life, which only exists in perpetual motion, as universal Becoming. This essential character of the living organism can only be fathomed through intuition, which gives us more than the senses and our consciousness, left to themselves, can achieve. Intuition is a strong mental effort of vision, which pierces the envelope of reality and opens the mind to the invisible side of materiality and, in particular, its evolution.

Bergson's belief in the dynamism of the universe leads him to develop a philosophy of movement and change. Change, he says, appears to us as a passage from one state to another. But it is wholly artificial trying to isolate states and to link them up like beads on a string, believing that this could be called movement. What we call a state is itself a change. Transition is always fluent, continuous, and constant. Movement is indivisible. We may indicate as many stopping places in the movement as we please. But movement itself cannot coincide with immobility; it cannot take a rest at any point in its trajectory, or it would cease to be movement.

From this, Bergson proceeds to a critique of our concept of time. There is a difference between our rational concept of time and the underlying reality of duration (which, again, can only be grasped through intuition and *then* explained through our intellect). Time is an arbitrary construction that cannot properly express the continuous movement of life. It is a static concept, whilst the essential quality of life is duration. Time is a product of the human intellect which approaches duration with a method derived from our spatialized concepts of reality. It seeks to make clean-cut distinctions and to divide into countable units what is in fact an indivisible process: duration. Time, therefore, is nothing but a bastard product of our mind, a phantom of space haunting our reflective consciousness.

Duration is continuity of mutually interpenetrating moments, with qualitative but not quantitative differentiations. Duration has no precise boundaries and cannot be divided into isolated elements. Qualitative changes permeate each other to such an extent that each 'element' is always a representation of the whole. Duration cannot be measured in numbers or units or any other quantitative representation of multiplicity. It is only the intellect that breaks up the uninterrupted flow of Being into artificial units and represents these successive states as homogeneous movement. Neither motion nor duration can be explained in spatialized terms. To do so (as science does) is equal to omitting their essential character: duration.

Bergson illustrates this concept of duration by drawing a parallel with a musical melody. A melody is essentially a unity, which owes its nature to change, but can only be what it is if one hears it in duration: 'If the melody stopped sooner it would no longer be the same sonorous whole'.[64]

---

[64] *Le Pensée et le mouvant* (Paris, 1934), p. 186. This quotation is taken from his lecture, *La Perception du changement*, given in Oxford in 1911.

In the same way, the permanent flux of the universe links every particle of reality to the rest. There are many qualitative changes; things die and are being reborn; but the universe as a whole endures. And if the universe exists in duration, so do we as human beings living in it. To exist is to change. To change is to grow. We participate in the universal flux and are part of the creation that never ceases.

This dynamic process of uninterrupted change, which constitutes the essence of life, cannot be apprehended rationally because life transcends intellect; but through intuition we gain consciousness of this eternal process. At every moment in time our personality is being built up through accumulating the experience of our ever-changing existence. Through our consciousness we create ourselves in every moment of our existence, and the more conscious we are of this process, the more complete is our self-creation. This conscious force is also called 'free will'. But freedom is not absolute. A decision to be free can only result from the action of gaining consciousness of our duration. It has to break through the artificial limits of time and other physical determinisms that prevent us from gaining consciousness of our mobility. Only when we act in defiance of the incrustations of reason and intellect, can we act according to our free will. Then, man is an agent rather than a spectator, so our inner life can be an active ingredient of the universal Becoming that we call progress, or evolution.

As we can see from this, Bergson's concepts of instinct and intuition are not mutually exclusive. He sees the development of creation as passing through three principle stages: from plants to animals to human beings. The first have no knowledge of reality, the second only an instinctive relation to it, but humans possess intellect *and* intuition. It is only when instinct reflects upon itself, when it becomes conscious of its force, that we receive the key to the vitality of life. Intuition alone (i. e. 'immediate consciousness' of reality), without the help of intellect (i. e. 'reflected consciousness'), remains riveted to the lower spheres of practical interests. It is tied to the material world and cannot 'speculate'. There are things which only the intellect is capable of seeking, but which, unaided, it cannot find. Only when instinct splits up into intuition and intelligence, and both operate in conjunction with one another, can we fully develop our creative potential and participate in the making of the universe. Instinct is the key to life, just as intellect is the key to the comprehension of life. When instinct purifies into intuition, and when intuition becomes conscious of itself (through intellect), we are set free from the slavery of (unconscious) action. We can move up and down the whole scale of Being, encompassing life and consciousness. Then the human mind coincides with the living principle from which it emanates, and we can develop our creative potential to perfection.

But what is this 'living principle' we come into contact with through intuition? It is the *élan vital*, the vital impulse, which is the key to the evolution of life in general. It is an impulsive energy that seeks to actualize itself in the material world, but encounters resistance from inert matter. Overcoming this resistance leads to successive transformations of life and to the development of higher levels of existence. Something of this original drive is preserved in all species and individual organisms, and all of them work unconsciously in its service. Life, like our consciousness, is infinitely inventive. By wrestling with the inertia of dead matter, new forms of life are incessantly created. By uncovering the workings of the vital impulse through intuition we can arrive at an understanding of life in the universe. Man as a creative genius mirrors the creativity and productivity of universal evolution. By participating in this process, man actualizes what the vital impulse has instilled in him as a potential. The virtual becomes actual and, through this, man makes himself. He becomes an artist (*homo faber*) and a philosopher (*homo sapiens*); mind and body work together; intellect and instinct operate in correlation. This new form of man is able to erect a new society.

The political philosophy of Liberalism, Revolutionary Syndicalism, and Anarchism

Bergson's writings were presented in an accomplished and poetical style and exercised a profound influence on many a writer. His philosophy captured the political climate of the New Age and gave expression to the way the modern world with its mobility and constant change was experienced by many artists of the period. His philosophy complemented and developed several aspects of Nietzsche's thinking. It is not astonishing, therefore, that both became philosophers *à la mode* at the turn of the century. Bergson's and Nietzsche's writings were not only discussed in literary circles, but their significance was also recognized by the political leaders of the Left and Right. Before I address myself to a closer analysis of one of these political philosophers, Georges Sorel, who became a lasting influence on Marinetti's ideological development, I should like to draw attention to some of the older theorists Marinetti had reason to study and admire.

When Marinetti first came to Paris, in 1894, he had only just begun to liberate himself from his early infatuation with positivism and naturalism. When he took his baccalaureate, he finished his philosophical studies with a 'triumphant exam on the theories of Stuart Mill'.[65] Marinetti does not say which of Mill's writings he had to study. Given the excellent results of the examination, there must have been something in Mill's thinking that appealed to him and made him read it over and over again. Whilst *Thoughts on Parliamentary Reform* (1859) and *Considerations on Representative Government* (1861) will have occupied him again later as a law student and, in particular, when he wrote his doctoral thesis on the topic of parliamentary democracy, his early enthusiasm for Mill is likely to have been prompted by *On Liberty* (1859), translated into French in 1860 as *La Liberté*.

Mill's political philosophy will have appealed to Marinetti as a manifesto of individualism. Mill took the 1793 Declaration of Human Rights and Tocqueville's reasonings on *Democracy in America* as a basis for erecting a system of thought that had at its centre the free individual, who had emancipated himself from custom and tradition and was at liberty to pursue his own interests in defiance of the

---

[65] Marinetti, *Marinetti e il futurismo* (Rome, 1929), in TeI 505.

'levelling' influences exercised by the masses. Mill preferred individual initiative to the 'paternalism of the State' the 'despotism of habit (which) is everywhere the standing hindrance of human advancement', and the 'opinions of the masses of merely average men' who seek to repress and regiment the 'pronounced individuality of those who stand on the higher eminences of thought'. For Mill, liberty was not only an individual but also a social good. To stifle it meant to rob society of the valuable contribution the 'free individual' could make to society. He was deeply suspicious of the parliamentarian forms of representation created by the older school of liberal politicians, and believed that practical politics had turned their government into a régime of mediocrity.

If Mill's early thinking was still heavily influenced by the ideals of the French Revolution, his later works — like *On Liberty* — were written in opposition to Marxist and socialist thinking. Mill represented bourgeois thinking after the seizure of power from the aristocracy. The principle of liberty had served the bourgeoisie as a weapon in the fight against the political restrictions of feudal society. It had established the position of the capitalist producer in a market economy and had challenged the domination of the status-bound landowning classes. This process served as the basis for a political philosophy of liberalism, which was first directed against any unnecessary interference from the State, and then, following the confrontation with the new social forces of the 'Fourth Estate', against the socialist/communist attempt to attain representation for the masses. By protecting the bourgeois ideals of 'Liberty, Equality, Fraternity' against the proletariat, these principles were turned upside down and given a direction that stood in marked contrast to their original intention: liberty became the liberty of an oligarchic élite; equality was replaced with inequality between the 'talented' and the 'mediocre' sections of society; and fraternity turned into competition between individual producers. The spectre of socialist collectivism led Mill to propagate a reign of the exceptional and original geniuses over the 'average of mankind', 'collective mediocrity', the 'mechanical' and 'dead matter'. His technocratic government of a bourgeois élite was a political expression of an anthropology which Marinetti will have interpreted as an advocation of an *Übermensch* cult:

> There are but a few persons, in comparison with the whole of mankind, whose experiments, if adopted by others, would be likely to be any improvement on established practice. But these few are the salt of the earth; without them, human life would become a stagnant pool. [...] Persons of genius, it is true, are, and are always likely to be, a small minority; but in order to have them, it is necessary to preserve the soil in which they grow. [...] If they are of strong character, and break their fetters, they become a mark for the society which has not succeeded in reducing them to commonplace, to point at with solemn warning as 'wild', 'erratic,' and the like. [...] I insist thus emphatically on the importance of genius. [...] Originality is the one thing which unoriginal minds cannot feel the use of. [...] At present individuals are lost in the crowd. In politics it is almost a triviality to say that public opinion now rules the world. The only power deserving the name is that of masses, and of governments while they make themselves the organ of the tendencies and instincts of masses. [...] No government by a democracy or a numerous aristocracy, either in its political acts or in the opinions, qualities, and tone of mind which it fosters, ever did or could rise above mediocrity, except in so far as the sovereign. Many

have let themselves be guided [...] by the counsels and influence of a more highly gifted and instructed One or Few. [...] Precisely because the tyranny of opinion is such as to make eccentricity a reproach, it is desirable, in order to break through that tyranny, that people should be eccentric. [...] Eccentricity in a society has generally been proportional to the amount of genius, mental vigour, and moral courage it contained. [...] The general average of mankind are not only moderate in intellect, but also moderate in inclinations: they have no tastes or wishes strong enough to incline them to do anything unusual, and they consequently do not understand those who have.[66]

The same autonomy of the creative genius from all principles of authority and the levelling forces of society became a fundamental element of Marinetti's nonconformist striving for total liberty. What Mill developed in moderation, Marinetti — influenced by various other sources — later took to its extreme. Ugo Piscopo, in his essay on *Marinetti and Positivism*,[67] argues that Marinetti also embraced the theories of Herbert Spencer, whose continuation and amplification of Mill's works was very much *en vogue* in France in the 1870s and 80s. In Spencer's works he could find an even more passionate defence of individualism and a denunciation of the 'slavery of socialism'[68] and of the political institution of parliamentary democracy. Spencer's fight against bureaucracy and gerontocracy was combined with an enthusiastic belief in a new future. He held that history progressed from a feudal society, where everybody had a fixed and stable status, to a dynamic capitalist society, which in its final phase would eliminate the institution of the State and replace laws with the use of contracts as the sole regulator of human life. He was a Social Darwinist through and through and believed in the self-made man who would rise to self-fulfilment by overcoming all biological and social obstacles. For Spencer, the natual evolution of mankind and of industrial society would successively weed out the unfit and eventually produce a race of supermen.

However, there is no firm evidence that Marinetti ever studied or read Spencer. We are, therefore, on much firmer ground with a political thinker Marinetti continued to read and discuss and who was a permanent point of reference in his political manifestos and the essays collected in *Democrazia futurista* (1919): Georges Sorel, the leading theoretician of Revolutionary Syndicalism, whose

---

[66] All quotations are taken from the chapter, 'On individuality, as one of the elements of well-being'.
[67] 'Marinetti e il positivismo', in Ugo Piscopo, *Questioni e aspetti del futurismo* (Naples, 1976), pp. 73–192.
[68] Herbert Spencer, *The Man Versus the State*, first published in *The Contemporary Review* (February to July 1884), then in book form in London in 1884. The first French edition, *L'Individu contre l'état*, appeared in 1885 (a fourth edition in 1895). It must, however, be said that the terms 'socialistic' and 'communistic' in the chapter on 'The Coming Slavery' do not denote modern socialism. When Spencer speaks of 'State-socialism' and 'All socialism involves slavery', he also applies this to the paternalistic and regulative policies of 'practical politicians' such as the Tories and Bismarck and not only to the 'tyranny of organizations' such as the Trade Unions.

anarchist rather than socialist orientation was particularly influential in Northern Italy.[69]

In the last quarter of the nineteenth century, the socialist movement in France had split up into political and economic wings operating quite independently of each other. The first was represented by the Socialist Party, which participated in the machinery of parliamentary democracy and even entered into government, whilst the second was a trade union movement, which was strictly reserved to representing the workers' economic and professional interests. The separation of the economic and the political fight, of parliament and the workshop floor, led the Socialist Party into an evermore revisionist position, much to the disappointment of the radical workers.

Out of this grew the syndicalist movement who, disenchanted with the politics of the Socialist Party, sought once again to integrate the political and economic struggle. One of their theoreticians was Fernand Pelloutier (1867–1901), first a militant socialist, then an anarchist.[70] In 1895, he became secretary of the *Fédération des bourses du travail*, and in his numerous articles outlined a rudimentary theory of syndicalism. His posthumously published *Histoire des bourses du travail* (1902) became a bible of the syndicalist movement.

According to his theory, the workers ought to use their organizations to undermine capitalism. The *syndicats* and *bourses* were seen not only as instruments for the protection of workers' professional interests, but as weapons to be employed systematically in the overthrow of the whole political system. Pelloutier's syndicalist theory was a critique of the political objectives of the reformist Socialist Party and of other groups committed either to democratic or insurrectionary seizure of State power. Pelloutier believed that any revolution that was not the result of the direct actions of the workers themselves would inevitably lead to the re-establishment of a hierarchical and authoritarian structure of society.

Pelloutier mistrusted parliamentary representation or the delegation of the fight for working-class emancipation to a revolutionary avant-garde. His political aim was not to reform the political system of the time, but to eradicate capitalism and abolish the State. But how could this objective be achieved?

---

[69] On French syndicalism see Frederic Ferdinand Ridley, *Revolutionary Syndicalism in France: The Direct Action of Its Time* (Cambridge, 1970); Jacques Juillard, *Autonomie ouvrière: Etudes sur le syndicalisme d'action directe* (Paris, 1988); Jeremy Jennings, *Syndicalism in France: A Study of Ideas* (Houndmills, 1990). On its influence in Italy see Osvaldo Gnocchi-Viani, *Le borse del lavoro* (Alessandria, 1889); Roberto Michels, *Storia critica del movimento socialista: Dagli inizi fino al 1911* (Florence, 1926); Dora Marucco, *Arturo Labriola e il sindacalismo rivoluzionario in Italia* (Turin, 1970); Alceo Riosa, *Il sindacalismo rivoluzionario in Italia e la lotta politica nel Partito Socialista dell'età giolittiano* (Bari, 1976); Gian Biagio Furiozzi, *Il sindacalismo rivoluzionario italiano* (Milan, 1977); David D. Roberts, *The Syndicalist Tradition and Italian Fascism* (Manchester, 1979). See also Antonio Toldo, *Il sindacalismo italiano* (Milan, 2nd edn, 1953) and Giorgio Candeloro, *Il movimento sindacale in Italia* (Rome, 1950).

[70] See Jacques Juillard, *Fernand Pelloutier et les origines du syndicalisme d'action directe* (Paris, 1971) and Alan B. Spitzer, 'Anarchy and Culture: Fernand Pelloutier and the Dilemma of Revolutionary Syndicalism', in *International Review of Social History*, 8 (1963), 379–88.

First of all, society had to be based on the free and voluntary association of producers, the *syndicats* and the *bourses du travail*. Whilst the *syndicats* were libertarian organizations controlling production, the *bourses* were the cells out of which the future society would grow. Both the *bourses* and *syndicats* formed a federalist association that served to foster the emancipation of the working class. Whilst the *syndicats* controlled the production process and reorganized it according to libertarian principles, the *bourses* anticipated a new social order. They offered mutual benefit and support structures, but also functioned as places of education and propaganda.

Through the *bourses* and *syndicats* the working classes would prepare themselves for the revolution. In order to avoid any bloodshed, Pelloutier advocated various peaceful means of subverting the capitalist State. Sabotage and strikes were to be employed in the obstruction of the smooth running of the industrial machine. The final overthrow of the capitalist system would be accomplished by a General Strike, which was seen as the safest and most efficient form of revolutionary action. Whilst the army could easily suppress a few thousand insurgents on the barricades, they were helpless against a widespread strike in thousands of factories which would paralyse the whole country and bring down the government.

Pelloutier's Revolutionary Syndicalism was a programme of action without a highly developed political theory. Sorel sought to rectify this by providing the movement with a new concept of society and economy.[71] Sorel had started his political career as a Jaurèsian socialist. When he became disappointed with the French Socialist Party, he moved towards an anarchist position. He had always been more inclined towards Proudhon than to Marx. In his 'Essai sur la philosophie de Proudhon'[72] he followed Proudhon's 'anarchist' vision of society in two main points: a) that society and economy should be based on small productive units, which form voluntary associations and co-operatives and replace State government; b) that the organization of a good and just society depends on positive action, struggle and war. Heroic combat is a principle condition of life and determines the strength and health of society.

Sorel developed a theory that distinguished between a socialism of producers, Party socialism and State socialism. In his view, only working-class socialism arising from the experience of the workshop floor was true socialism, whilst the other forms were compromises with the capitalist system. Sorel had become extremely disappointed with the development of 'social democracy' in France and Germany. After Millerand's entry into Waldeck-Rousseau's cabinet (1899) it became clear to him that a Socialist Party participating in a bourgeois government would by necessity become corrupted and eventually swallowed up in the 'democratic ocean'.[73] The Dreyfus Affair had proved to him the deceitfulness and dishonesty of the governing classes and the corrupt state of liberal democracy. If

[71] See Peter Schöttler, '"La Commune ouvrière en formation"? Georges Sorel et les bourses du travail', in *Georges Sorel en son temps*, ed. by J. Juillard and S. Sand (Paris, 1985), pp. 53–73.
[72] In *Revue philosophique*, 33 (1892), 622–38 and 34 (1892), 41–68.
[73] Sorel, *Matériaux d'une théorie du prolétariat* (Paris, 1919), p. 263.

socialism was to preserve its historical mission, it had to make a clean break with the bourgeoisie, with democracy, and with the parliamentarian system. Whilst the leaders of the Socialist Party believed that a democratic attitude could be used to the advantage of the working class, Sorel regarded this as pure illusion. He believed that there could be no co-existence of democracy and socialism, because they represented two mutually opposing class interests. 'The city of tomorrow must be organized apart from democratic ideas. Social classes must be marshalled in spite of and against democracy. We must re-awaken class-consciousness stifled at present by democratic ideas.'[74]

Therefore, an autonomous, genuine workers' organization had to be set up against the Socialist Party, which had become as unscrupulous as the bourgeois politicians. The leadership of compromise (Jaurès, Guesde and Millerand) had to be replaced with a directorate of the People. In *L'Avenir socialiste des syndicats* (1898), Sorel devised a programme for a self-government of workers' organizations. The *syndicats* and *bourses* represented the 'new political principle of the proletariat', where the abstract citizen was replaced by a worker and the political arena by a factory.[75]

In order to examine the production process and to probe Marxism in depth, Sorel began to study economics and thereby arrived at a fundamental re-interpretation of the Marxist tradition in socialist thinking. He sought to return to the spirit of Marx's writings, which he believed to contain some valuable elements of early socialist utopianism. This original energy of revolt, he thought, could be salvaged for the revolutionary working class, but only if Marx's determinist belief in the ultimate socialist victory was repealed. Sorel believed that real change could only be achieved through class struggle. The Socialists' faith in the inevitability of progress had sapped their moral energy and had led to a kind of social quietism. Sorel rejected their politics of reform, transformation, and evolution and argued that the proletariat had to trust in their ability to combat for the conquest of power and to shape their own future through revolutionary action.

The underlying premise of Sorel's philosophy of violence was a mixture of Nietzschean and Bergsonian[76] assumptions on life and human activity. War was seen as a fundamental motive behind human action, whilst pacifism was regarded as a form of cowardice. Heroism and risk-taking were interpreted as an expression of a fundamental attitude to life, and social revolution as a natural consequence of the engrained characteristics of the human race. Without the *élan vital* there could be no dynamic evolution of the world; without class war there would be no progress through history.

[74] Sorel, *Lettre sur "La Cité française"*, in A. Lanzarillo, 'G. Sorel e i monarchici francesi contro la democrazia', in *Giornale d'Italia*, 20 November 1910.
[75] See 'L'avenir socialiste des syndicats', in *Matériaux*, pp. 118–19.
[76] Sorel had read Bergson in the early 1890s, but only after 1900, when he heard some of Bergson's lectures at the Collège de France, did he come under the influence of the French philosopher. On the relation between the two see Pierre Andreu, *Bergson et Sorel* (Paris, 1952).

Sorel's 'violence' was not, as was later often misunderstood, an appeal to terrorist bloodshed. Rather it was a metaphysical principle which found expression in any form of struggle. He saw it as a creative force that could be active in artists, inventors, and warriors imbued with individuality and originality and, therefore, a revolutionary mentality.

However, this metaphysical force, even if it is intuitively recognized by the individual, can only become an active force in life when the impediments of the existing order are overcome. This is where 'effort' translates into revolt, 'élan' into battle. It is political activity driven by 'creative hatred'. It has nothing to do with brutality and certainly should not repeat the carnage of the 'year of terror', 1793. Sorel's revolutionary method is the General Strike, which takes on a mythical dimension in his writings of this period. 'As long as there are no myths accepted by the masses, one may go on talking of revolts indefinitely, without ever provoking any revolutionary change. This is what gives such importance to the General Strike, [...] the only idea that can have any value as a motive force.'[77] It is for him 'concentrated class struggle' (*lutte de classe concentrée*) and 'the test by which workers' socialism distinguishes itself from amateur revolutionaries'.[78] Sorel offers an 'application of Bergson's ideas to the theory of the General Strike'[79] and distinguishes between 'analytical reflection' (i. e. rational education though the *bourses*) and the effect myths have on the workers' intuitive faculty and revolutionary sentiments:

> The General Strike is [...] the myth which encapsulates the whole idea of socialism. It is a body of images capable of evoking instinctively all the feelings that correspond to the diverse manifestations of the battle for socialism. [...] Thereby we obtain that intuition of socialism which language cannot give us with perfect clearness, and we obtain it as a whole in a moment of instant perception.[80]

But Sorel was also influenced by Nietzschean thought. This is where the cult of the hero entered his political philosophy. Sorel emphasized the need of the proletarian masses for a leader. He is an exemplary figure who concentrates in himself the universal virtues of a *condottiero* and messiah. He unleases in the proletariat the fighting instinct and leads them to the victorious conclusion of the social revolution. The hero has in himself the intuitive *élan vital* and the *Wille zur Macht*,[81] which are ultimately responsible for social progress. In that respect, Sorel's notion of class struggle came closer to Nietzsche's and Bergson's philosophy

---

[77] Sorel, *Réflexions sur la violence*, 3rd edn (Paris, 1912), pp. 233 and 169. On page 180 he defines it as a 'moyen d'agir sur le présent' and 'un élément de force de premier ordre', which gives 'à l'ensemble des pensées révolutionnaires une précision et une raideur que n'auraient pu leur fournir d'autre manières de penser'.

[78] Ibid., p. 45.

[79] Ibid., p. 174, note 1.

[80] Ibid., p. 182. The same idea is expressed on page 173: 'Le langage ne saurait suffire pour produire de tels résultats d'une manière assurée; il faut faire appel à des ensembles d'images capables d'évoquer en bloc et par la seule intuition, avant toute analyse réfléchie, la masse des sentiments qui correspondent aux diverses manifestations de la guerre engagée par le socialisme."

[81] Both the Bergsonian and Nietzschean terms are used in *Réflexions sur la violence*; see in particular, p. 224.

than to Marx' materialist analysis. And, in fact, the typical hero Sorel had in mind was not necessarily a worker, but could also be a capitalist entrepreneur. Sorel was far from promoting an agrarian idyll according to Proudhon's model. In his view, the workers and the socialist movement must accept the heritage of capitalist industry. Modern industry is the productive force of the future. The capitalist who fulfils his productive tasks makes a vital contribution to the building of the *cité* of the future. He is not a *rentier* like the majority of the decaying élite in France. And he is more productive than the State socialists, whose *étatisme* has a stifling influence on the workers. State socialism is the rule of mediocrity and leads to a false democracy, which is more hierarchical and élitist than the aristocratic régime it pretends to replace. The democratic system has only achieved over-centralization, a hypertrophic growth of bureaucracy and the rule of inefficient managers over producers. True socialism therefore has to be anti-democratic. It will create a healthy community by transforming every individual into an active producer. Sorel's Revolutionary Syndicalism is, in the final analysis, an organi-zation of heroic individuals, of an élite of the productive classes, who have a historic mission to fulfil: to restore vitality to a dying civilization.

Sorel's political theory was not only of influence amongst the French working class disenchanted with the Socialist leadership. It had an immediate impact on the Italian syndicalist movement, and — via a vulgarized interpretation — on Fascism in its germinal phase.[82] It also found a positive reception amongst large sections of the anarchist movement, and fell on fertile ground amongst the bohemian intellec-tuals of the period who had always despised the bourgeois ethos of the Socialist Party.

Anarchism was not only a political ideology and was certainly not in the first instance a working-class phenomenon. It was firmly entrenched amongst impov-erished writers and artists, declassé intellectuals and the bohemian population of Montmartre.[83] It represented a wide-ranging cultural rebellion, a critique of bourgeois values, State power and all hallowed traditional institutions. For this reason it was widely diffused through the milieu of avant-garde artists, who tried to combine political with artistic radicalism.

Le Matin of 9 March 1894 estimated that in Paris there were about 500 anarchists;[84] significantly, a police report of 1890 only mentions 47 anarchist

---

[82] It is worth pointing out that some of Sorel's writings appeared in Italy before their publication in France. He was certainly better known, and more widely read, in Italy than in his home country. This, at least, was Croce's opinion expressed in his preface to the Italian edition of Sorel's *Considerazioni sulla violenza* (Bari, 1909). On Italian *sorelismo* see Gian Biagio Furiozzi, *Sorel e l'Italia* (Messina, 1975). On its influence on early Fascism see Jack Roth, 'The Roots of Italian Fascism: Sorel and Sorelismo', in *Journal of Modern History*, 39 (1967), 30–45; Michel Charzat, 'Georges Sorel et le fascisme: Eléments d'explication d'une légende tenace', in *Cahiers Georges Sorel*, 1 (1983), 37–52; Giuseppe L. Goisis, *Sorel e i Soreliani* (Venice, 1983); Sergio Romano, 'Sorel e Mussolini', in *Storia contemporanea*, 15 (1984), 123–31; Roberto Vivarelli, 'Georges Sorel et le fascisme', in Juillard & Sand, *Georges Sorel en son temps*, pp. 123–33.
[83] See Richard D. Sonn, *Anarchism and Cultural Politics in Fin de Siècle France* (Lincoln, Nebraska, 1989).
[84] See Sonn, *Anarchism and Cultural Politics*, p. 57.

militants in the working-class *banlieu*.[85] With the exception of *La Révolte*, every major anarchist journal in the 1890s was edited and published in Montmartre. The police records show that there was a dense anarchist activity in this quarter, which centred on cafés, cabarets, music halls, local *Maisons du Peuple*, etc. and attracted between 200 and 300 visitors to each meeting. A detailed police report on the *café concert* run by Maxime Lisbonne called the place a 'socialist-anarchist centre' with a 'politico-literary clientele'.[86] Another report described the Théâtre de l'Œuvre as 'an anarchist literary society'.[87]

When Marinetti was staying in Paris, he had plenty of opportunity to study anarchism. There is reason to believe that his conversion to the Symbolist school was not only motivated by aesthetic considerations, but also strongly influenced by the radical political viewpoints advocated by the movement. In 1893, *L'Ermitage* asked a representative number of writers about their political allegiances, and found that anarchist sentiments were wide-spread amongst the Symbolists.[88] Gustave Kahn, Marinetti's discoverer and mentor, introduced his young disciple to many political artists and activists who subsequently exercised considerable influence on his early poetic and dramatic output, and who served as animating spirits for his Futurist vision of a new art and society.

It is well-known, for example, that Alfred Jarry had close contacts with the anarchist circles of Montmartre. In 1903, Kahn introduced him, at the offices of *La Revue blanche*, to the up-and-coming Italian poet.[89] Marinetti never mentions having seen the original production of *Ubu Roi* in 1896 or reading the text when it appeared in June 1896. But in his memoirs he refers to Jarry with great affection:

> I can see myself now with Alfred Jarry in the ornate salon of Mme Périer where from three to eleven at night thirty or forty men and women spouting poetry would parade [...] I toss off my ode on the speed of cars and Jarry his metamorphosis of a bus into an elephant.[90]

When in Italy, Marinetti kept in contact with Jarry.[91] In one letter of July 1906, Jarry thanked him for having been sent a copy of Marinetti's first major play, *Le Roi Bombance,* published a few months earlier by *Le Mercure de France*, and said:

> It's a long time since we last saw each other at the *Mercure*. I'm saying this to excuse my delayed reply. I have read *Le Roi Bombance* for a second time now, and it still provokes the same vivid impression, because of its extraordinary form and precision of language. [...] The play is an admirable novelty [...]. You have offered what no doubt only you could have produced, i.e. the twilight of this God in the superb apotheosis of Saint

---

[85] Ibid., p. 56.
[86] Ibid., p. 68.
[87] Ibid., p. 54.
[88] See Marco de Micheli, *La matrice ideologico-letteraria dell'eversione fascista* (Milan, 1976), p. 18.
[89] On the *Revue blanche* and its circle see the studies by A. B. Jackson, *La Revue blanche (1889–1903): Origine, influence, bibliographie* (Paris, 1960) and Georges Bernier, *La Revue blanche: Ses amis, ses artistes* (Paris, 1991).
[90] *Una sensibilità italiana*, pp. 244–45 (Flint 330–31). The poem which Marinetti recited here and on a number of other occasions (see *La grande Milano*, pp. 73 and 84), was 'A mon Pégase', published in *Poesia* in the same year. See below p. 75.
[91] See Alfred Jarry, *Œuvres complètes*, 3 (Paris, 1988), 635 f., 978 f., and 2 (Paris, 1987), 801–02.

Putrefaction. [...] Glory again to Bombance, the good King, for all the joy he has given me.[92]

Le Roi Bombance was modelled in many ways on Jarry's *Ubu Roi*: it contains the same onslaught on theatrical high culture through its use of devices taken from popular traditions of theatre; the outrageously violent plot has many similarities with Ubu's exploits; there is the same anarchic undertone in the play, a quest for freedom and individual fulfilment, an exaltation of rebellion, a call for the overthrow of the established order, a scorning of corruption, religious hypocrisy and false moral values. In short, it possesses all the 'dynamic vivacity of a new Futurist theatricality' Marinetti called for in the *Synthetic Theatre Manifesto* of 1915,[93] and there can be no doubt that Jarry gave Marinetti important inspiration in that field.

The dramatic shock-tactics of *Le Roi Bombance* were complemented by Marinetti's increasingly anarchical and iconoclastic poetry, some of which was published, in 1904, in a book entitled *Destruction* (see below, pp. 48–55). Several of the works in this collection were dedicated to anarchist friends in Paris. One of them was Paul Adam, editor of *Entretiens politiques et littéraires*, a magazine which promoted an interesting mixture of modernism in poetry and radicalism in politics.[94] Marinetti dedicated his first published play, *Le Roi Bombance* to Adam, and remembered him in his memoirs, saying: 'My imagination hungered for new literary forms and was nourished by Paul Adam's friendship'.[95] Also Henri de Régnier, whom Marinetti singled out in the notebooks of his student years and to whom he dedicated one of the Dithyrambs published in *Poesia* (August 1905), was an anarchist and a regular contributor to Adam's *Entretiens*, as was Laurent Tailhade, dedicatee of the most anarchist poem in *Destruction* (1904): *Hymne à la mort*.

From the second half of the 1890s onwards, the French anarchists became closely allied to the syndicalist movement.[96] Many radical intellectuals followed this trend and embraced a new form of politics that fell somewhere between the categories of syndicalism, socialism, and communism. Poinsot judged in 1907: 'Most Symbolists tended politically towards anarchism, which is understandable given their extreme individualism. However, the new recruits and the sober ones of the previous period embraced the altruistic doctrine of socialism'.[97]

---

[92] The letter is included in Jarry, *Œuvres complètes*, III, 635–36. An Italian translation was published by Marinetti in *Poesia* nos 9–12 (October 1907–January 1908) and reprinted in S. Lambase & G. B. Nazzaro, *F. T. Marinetti Futurista* (Naples, 1977), pp. 329–31. The date of the letter is missing in the Italian version. Viazzi, following the Dossier 25 of the Institutum Pataphysicum Mediolanense (3 March 1964), pp. 22–23, suggests winter 1905/06 for the letter, but the editor of the *Œuvres Complètes*, who used the original manuscript in the Marinetti papers at Yale University, dates it 31 July 1906.

[93] Tel 104, Flint 128.

[94] See Thierry Maricourt, *Histoire de la littérature libertaire en France* (Paris, 1990), p. 81 and Jean Grave, *Quarante ans de propagande anarchiste* (Paris, 1973), p. 344.

[95] *Una sensibilità italiana*, p. 223 (Flint 318).

[96] See Jean Maitron, *Le Mouvement anarchiste en France*, I (Paris, 1975), 263–330.

[97] Maffeo-Charles Poinsot, *Littérature sociale* (Paris, 1907), p. 56.

The Abbaye de Créteil, Jules Romains and Unanimism

One of the most important artistic phenomena to illustrate this trend was the foundation, in 1906, of the Abbaye de Créteil,[98] which two of the founding fathers described as a 'Communistic'[99] and a 'Bolshevik'[100] experiment. The socialist vision that inspired the members of this 'artists' commune' was principally derived from Proudhon and Tolstoy. The estate, some ten miles south-east of Paris, accommodated a self-sufficient *groupe fraternel des artistes*, who practised their art and craft in a manner that escaped the corruption and commercialism of the bourgeois art market. Three of the founding members had previously been involved with the running of the *Association Ernest Renan* and had received valuable inspiration from Gustave Kahn's *Samedis populaires* and the *Universités populaires*.[101] They now continued to pursue their aim of bringing art to the people, of educating the masses and regenerating their spiritual condition through art and literature.[102] The Abbaye was to be a model for the society of the future, where art would be integrated into communal living, where productive associations were formed by 'free spirits', and where everyone 'lived in the ardor of achievement supported by a perfect communion.'[103] Despite the rather idyllic surroundings of the Abbaye, the members of the commune did not renounce their interest in the modern city, the machine, and the psychology of the masses.[104] The works produced and exhibited at the Abbaye were firmly linked with the experience of modernity. Although situated outside Paris, the fraternity sustained a close contact with the artistic community of the capital.

[98] On the Abbaye de Créteil see Daniel Robbins, 'From Symbolism to Cubism: The Abbaye of Créteil', in *Art Journal*, 23 (1963–64), 111–16.
[99] Albert Gleizes, 'The Abbey of Créteil, a Communistic Experiment', in *The Modern School* (Stelton, New Jersey, October 1918), pp. 300–15.
[100] Alexandre Mercereau, *L'Abbaye et le bolchevisme* (Paris s. d. [1922]).
[101] See *Albert Gleizes, 1881–1953: Exposition rétrospective*, Paris: Musée national d'art moderne (1964–65), p. 13.
[102] See Gilbert Guisan, *Poésie et collectivité, 1890–1914: Le message social des oeuvres poétiques de l'unanimisme et de l'Abbaye* (Paris, 1938). Georges Duhamel, in his autobiography *Lumières sur ma vie. Vol. 3: Le temps de la recherche* (Paris, 1947), plays down the social content of their 'projets [d'ivresse], des constructions aériennes, des visions édéniques' (p. 30) and states categorically: 'On a vu, on a cru voir dans l'aventure de l'Abbaye une expérience de caractère politique. La belle affaire! A vrai dire, nous ignorions les doctrinaires du collectivisme; nous n'avions lu que Rabelais, Vallès, Rimbaud, les poètes, surtout les poètes. Nous ne cherchions sûrement pas un remède général aux misères de la société; nous ne pensions qu'aux hommes de notre condition [i. e. artists and intellectuals, G.B.]' (p. 42). Corresponding with his later deprecation of the experiment, he wrote a highly satirical novel on the Abbaye experience, *Le Désert de Bièvre* (1937). Gleizes's memoirs in *The Modern School* do not support Duhamel's contention. For a contemporary visitor's reactions see Noël Amaudru, 'Voyages en Icarie: Les poètes du socialisme, du rêve à la réalité, L'Abbaye de Créteil', in *xıxème siècle* (Paris), 23 November 1907.
[103] Gleizes, 'The Abbaye de Créteil', p. 307. However, he admitted that 'our anarchist tendencies, our independences, so imperious, did not bend easily to discipline, as such an affair required.' (Ibid.).
[104] See Daniel Robbins' introduction to the Gleizes catalogue of 1964–65.

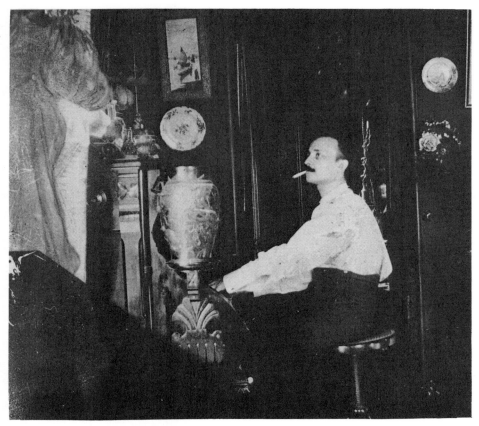

FIG. 4.   Marinetti in his flat, playing the harmonium

In their memoirs, Duhamel and Gleizes mention a large number of cultural activities organized by the Abbaye circle. Albert Doyen began at Créteil some of his vast choral compositions, and the musical setting of Vildrac's lyrical drama, *L'Apothéose*. His wife Rachel, a well-known singer and musician, had accompanied him to the Abbaye, where she performed excerpts from several of these new compositions. Other evenings were dedicated to poetry readings, dramatic recitations by visiting actors and actresses, and performances of short plays or scenes in a specially constructed theatre in the park. A whole arts festival was set up so that 'people could see us actually at work, become interested in our enterprise'.[105] Occasionally, they organized exhibitions of paintings and sculptures of, amongst others, Jacques d'Otémar, Gabriel Pinta, Maurice Drouard, Constantin Brancusi, and Umberto Brunelleschi.

[105] Gleizes, 'The Abbaye of Créteil', p. 311.

We know that Marinetti was a regular guest at the Abbaye and derived considerable profit from the contacts established there. Barzun, who had financed the whole enterprise, became a great admirer of Futurism and sang Marinetti's praise in several essays of his journal *Poème et drame*. Mercereau, who spent a lot of his time in Russia, organized Marinetti's spectacular tour of Moscow and St Petersburg in 1914. It also was in Créteil that Marinetti first met the poetess Valentine de Saint-Point, who later joined the Futurist movement and penned the influential *Manifesto of the Futurist Woman*.

But amongst all these new acquaintances and friendships formed in Créteil one affords special mention: Jules Romains. He was a Jaurèsian socialist, who believed that industrial development would have a strengthening effect on social solidarity. His experience of the big city had been overwhelmingly positive and had generated an optimistic view of urban life, which he traced back to an experience in 1903 when, walking down the crowded Rue d'Amsterdam, he was suddenly seized by a vision of the whole city merging into one vast cohesive unity.[106] Intuitively, he had gained access to the collective consciousness of an urban conglomeration.

The following year, he published a first collection of poems under the aegis of the Société des Poètes Français, containing *La Ville consciente*, an evocative description of modern city life. His vision of the new mentality, developed by urban collectives, became even clearer in *Le Poème du métropolitain* of 1905, an extended prose poem written partly in *vers libres* and depicting a journey on the Paris subway. The decidedly 'modern' topic of technological advance in the everyday life of a Big City dweller was combined with a psychological analysis of the groups and collectives formed by the industrial environment.

Underlying these first poems and a couple of short stories published in the same year was a philosophy which he first called communism[107] and then changed to 'unanimism'. It is based on Romains' own personal experience of pulsating city life and the way it welds people together into groups and communities that are fundamentally different from those of the pre-industrial age.

Unanimism is a concept of group consciousness that can only be found in the modern metropolis. It describes a psychic concord in a collective where the individual's personality merges with that of others, and this interpenetration of states of mind creates a powerful, all-encompassing group identity, which is qualitatively different from that of the sum of its particles. The *unanime* is a representative feature of contemporary life and can be found in crowded streets, offices or factories. Once modern man has grown conscious of this new reality, a collective power develops that is superhuman and divine. The fusion of various *unanimes* creates a *unité superieure* that will lead to a new humanity where all mankind is synthetized into a total being with divine quality. They become a *dieu*, a universal or world-god.

---

[106] The experience has been reported in André Cuisenier, *Jules Romains et l'unanimisme* (Paris, 1935), p. 17.

[107] See André Cuisenier and René Maublanc, 'Introduction', in Georges Chennevière, *Œuvres poétiques* (Paris, 1929), pp. 29–30.

Romains' first major publication, *La Vie unanime*, brought him, at the age of twenty-two, immediate fame in the Parisian literary world. The book was written between 1904 and 1907 and printed in 1908 by the collective of the Abbaye de Créteil. An enthusiastic review appeared in Marinetti's magazine, *Poesia*, in the number of September 1908, following the publication of other examples and reviews of Romains's verses in September 1906, January 1907 and July 1908.

It is worth analysing *La Vie unanime* in more detail here, for it contains a number of features that are of great relevance to Marinetti's development of a Futurist aesthetics. The book contains 58 poems divided into six sections, which describe the author's progression towards an understanding and appreciation of the *unanime*. After a first experience of modern life in the metropolis the author discovers a gradual uneasiness and dislike of the *unanimes*. He rejects the city and flees into nature, only to find that this isolated country existence offers nothing but solitude and insecurity. He finally returns to the city and enters into a mystical communion with the *unanime*. The poems set in the metropolis evoke the hustle and bustle on the boulevards, the cafés, department stores, offices, and factories. There is a 'music of the masses' (p. 110), created by the city's 'feverish pulsations' (p. 135), the shouts of paper merchants, the noise, rhythm and dynamism of cars, lorries, trams and trains. He discovers the interpenetration of forms, shapes and colours and finds that this ensemble contains 'a harmony in flames and on the move' (une harmonie en flamme et en marche, p. 171). His eyes no longer see 'separate forms', but only the 'totality' of big city life (p. 159). This new state of mind is complemented by a an equally novel physical sensation: 'I abandon myself to the rhythm of the passers-by, the *unanime* quivers around my brain, the city becomes my body, undulating, trembling, burning, bursting with joy.'[108]

After the description of the disappointing experience in the heart of Nature, there follow three poems, entitled 'La conscience qui devient' (p. 224), 'Unanime, je t'aime' (p. 229) and 'Retour' (p. 232). The author is filled with a 'prophetic dream of unity' (p. 228), which he finds realized in the 'joyful crossroads of unanimous rhythms, a condenser of universal energy' (le carrefour joyeux des rhythmes unanimes, un condenseur de l'énergie universelle, p. 238). His heart feels an emotional upsurge ('une émotion incandescente', p. 239) and like Marinetti in his famous manifesto *Let's Kill the Moonshine*, Romains exclaims: 'Nous éblouirons le clair de lune.' (p. 239) The similarity to Marinetti's *vers libres* in the above-mentioned manifesto is even more apparent in the last section, which abounds with words such as noise, colours, light, flames, electricity, power, energy, vibration, rhythm, movement, and metaphors such as exploding volcanoes, the galloping towards the sky, the sun, the stars, etc.

As these quotes from Romains' cycle of poems reveal, there was a close similarity between the French poet's vision of life in the modern metropolis and Marinetti's Futurist aesthetics. It was through Marinetti that the painters who congregated in

---

108 'Je m'abandonne tout au rhythme des passants, l'unanime frémit autour de ma cervelle' (p. 165); 'la ville devient [...] mon corps, ondule, tremble, brûle, jouit' (p. 175).

his Milanese apartment in January/February 1910 learned about Unanimism. It proved to be of fundamental influence on their work which, until that date, had remained in the older painterly traditions of post-impressionism, divisionism, and art-nouveau. In his *Founding and Manifesto of Futurism*, Marinetti had provided them with a basic philosophy expressing a new attitude to the modern age. But his aesthetics had a predominently literary and poetic basis, which could not easily be applied to painting. As Marianne Martin has shown,[109] it was through Unanimism that the Futurist painters developed a new concept of the figurative arts, where interpenetration of shapes and colours and the device of simultaneity became central features. It is hardly surprising then that Apollinaire, when he reviewed the first Futurist exhibition in Paris in 1912, could remark that their works 'often appear to have been borrowed from the vocabulary of Unanimism.'[110]

Although Romains did not belong to the inner circle of the Abbaye de Créteil community,[111] it seems relevant to the context of our argument here that his poems were seen as representative of the modern spirit the community sought to encapsulate in their experiment. The Abbaye group was conceived as an *unanime* and as a model of the society they envisaged for the future. Set up in opposition to the restraints of bourgeois society and the limitations of traditional artistic practice, creative activity was closely linked with communal living. The fusion of art and life in the Créteil co-operative made the commune famous throughout Europe. Artists from all over France and even abroad visited the Abbaye, participated in its literary soirées, festivals, and art exhibitions.

The experiment carried out at the Abbaye de Créteil between 1906 and 1908 left a lasting impression on Marinetti. The community of Créteil served as a model for his later attempts to break down the autonomous position of art in the bourgeois world and to fuse it with life as experienced in the modern age.[112] Marinetti's regular visits to Paris were clearly not only motivated by opportunistic considerations (i. e. the furthering of his career as a writer). France offered great stimulation and inspiration to him in terms of literary aesthetics, political concepts, and general *Weltanschauung*. Although not all of these sources were of French origin, it was in France and through French translations that Marinetti discovered some of the key figures who influenced his world view and aesthetic theories.

---

[109] Marianne W. Martin, 'Futurism, Unanimism and Apollinaire', in *Art Journal*, 28 (1969), 258–68, and in her volume *Futurist Art and Theory (1909–1915)*, Oxford 1968. See also Guy Taillade, 'Unanimisme, Futurisme, Abbaye de Créteil', in *Bulletin des amis de Jules Romains*, 7, no. 23 (March 1981), 15–25 and Marzio Pinottini, 'L'unanimismo e l'estetica del futurismo', in *Unanimismo Jules Romains*, ed. by P. A. Jannini & S. Zoppi (Rome/Paris, 1978), pp. 95–111.

[110] G. Apollinaire, 'Les peintres futuristes italiens', in *L'Intransigeant* (7 February 1912), reprinted in *Chroniques d'art*, ed. by L.-C. Breunig (Paris, 1960), p. 212; English edition: *Apollinaire on Art: Essays and Reviews 1902–1918* (New York, 1972), p. 199.

[111] See P. J. Norrish, 'Romains and L'Abbaye', in *Modern Language Review*, 52 (1957), 518–25.

[112] The influence of the Abbaye group and their sympathizers (André Ibels, Théo Varlet, P. J. Jouve, etc.) on Marinetti has been analysed by Mariani, *Preistoria del futurismo*, pp. 135–40; Michel Décaudin, *La Crise des valeurs symbolistes* (Toulouse, 1960), pp. 243–44; Bruno Romani, *Dal simbolismo al futurismo* (Florence, 1969), pp. 71–85. There was, of course, a large number of other French writers and poets to whom Marinetti was indebted in some way or other. The most significant influences have been discussed in the studies of Mariani and Romani.

FIG. 5. Marinetti as a declaimer of Symbolist poetry, *c.* 1902

Symbolism and the Art of Declamation

Finally, I should like to outline a further source of influence with which Marinetti came into contact in France and which shaped his notion of a modern, Futurist form of theatre and performance art. As a dramatist he emulated Jarry's attempts to activate his audience via the creation of outrageous characters on stage and the provocation of theatre scandals. But while in France he also launched his own career as a performer and developed an acting style that led smoothly into his later technique of 'Dynamic and Synoptical Declamation', which became a hallmark of the early Futurist *serate*.

Marinetti's first contact with the French art of declamation took place in 1898, when he was invited to Paris to receive his literary prize and to hear his

FIG. 6.   Marinetti declaiming his poetry from the bust of Alessandro Manzoni in the park of Viggiù

award-winning poem being recited by Sarah Bernhardt at Gustave Kahn's *Samedis populaires*. The event formed part of a regular series of matinée poetry readings and performances of plays written by young poets and playwrights. Kahn made a conscious attempt with his *samedis* to return poetry to its true domaine, that of public recitation, where voice and gesture transformed the printed word into live acts of the highest intensity.[113]

The public declamation of poetry in theatres appears to have been a popular art in late nineteenth-century France. Whole troupes specializing in the art of declamation toured France, reciting poems, old and new, to a wide array of audiences. Marinetti was fascinated by this type of performance, although he found that the style and form of declamation usually employed left a lot to be desired. Even Sarah Bernhardt's rendering of his own verses sounded, as he noted in his autobiography, 'a little monotonous due to her usual way of reciting alexandrines'.[114]

Of a different class altogether were the poetry evenings organized by the Grand Théâtre du Gymnase in Marseille. Attached to the theatre was a conservatory which specialized in teaching the art of declamation. One of the theatre's performance spaces was regularly used for poetry evenings, and in 1905 Marinetti was invited to present a selection of Italian and French poems. In a preceding talk he expressly condemned the traditional way in which the Comédie Française taught the art of declamation. He then surprised the Marseilles audience, which on this occasion was enlarged by a large contingent of Parisian high society who spent the summer months in the province, with a poetry reading that left them speechless. After the show he was fêted in a nearby restaurant and was beseeched to offer a few more specimens of his own writings. He remembers in his mémoirs:

> At the first booming out of my powerful voice they immediately demand that I recite standing on the table and so I push aside the still-hot platters full of bright oily fish scales and tails right into their liquor-glazed faces. Thin and elegant in my smoking jacket my shirt wringing wet and my collar twisted into its own anarchical freedom I begin thundering out and send motors roaring up up until they overshoot the Milky Way race course.[115]

Marinetti's appearances at the Théâtre du Gymnase and at Kahn's *Samedis populaires* did not remain isolated incidents. Having presented the latest Italian poets in France, he went on tour in Italy with an equally modern French repertoire, stocked up with many of his own poems and some audience shockers such as Laurent Tailhade's *Hymn to anarchy*.[116] Marinetti's experience of the audience's reaction to this kind of performance furnished him with the virtuosity and adroitness he could later draw on when he commenced his *serate* in 1910. He turned the art of declamation into a dynamic, controversial form of theatre, and there can be no doubt that his appearances at Kahn's *Samedis populaires* were a

---

[113] See Jacques Robichez, *Le Symbolisme au théâtre* (Paris, 1957), p. 391.

[114] *Una sensibilità italiana*, p. 243 (Flint 330).

[115] *Una sensibilità italiana*, p. 241 (Flint 326–27).

[116] See the review in the journal *Lombardia*, reprinted in Tullio Pànteo's biography *Il poeta Marinetti*, pp. 97–103.

first tangible expression of the performance style he cultivated with great effectiveness in his Futurist theatre events.

PART TWO

MARINETTI'S EARLY WORKS: A PRELUDE TO FUTURISM

Paolo Baglione

Marinetti's activities in the ten years between his graduation and the inception of the Futurist movement can be roughly divided into four categories: a) creative writing (poetry, prose, and drama); b) critical writing; c) editorial work; d) performances.

The first substantial play which survives from his early production is a juvenile drama in four acts, untitled, but sometimes referred to by the name of its protagonist, *Paolo Baglione*.[117] From a literary point of view this work is of little value, but it is worthy of analysis because of the contrast it offers to Marinetti's later dramatic experiments. *Paolo Baglione* is quite typical of the drama Marinetti polemicized against in his Futurist period: it contains a mixture of elements derived from Hugo and d'Annunzio; it has a romantic Venetian setting; it is a historical drama in so much as it deals with a fifteenth-century *coup d'état* against the aristocratic régime of the Republic. Set against public scenes full of dramatic movement are lyrical interludes, where the love between the protagonist Paolo and Rosalba is psalmodized.

The rather rickety plot revolves around the Condottiere Baglione, who has just returned victorious from a three-year war against the Turks, and a group of conspirators, who regard him as a tyrant and therefore want to dispose of him. The first act is set in front of Baglione's palace next to the Arsenale. After a ten year construction period, the great State ship, Fortunata, has just been finished and is about to be baptized by the hero of the Republic. All dignitaries of the Senate are present; but when they are about to launch the ship, they find out that the scaffolding has been tampered with in order to produce an accident. The launch has to be postponed, and the suspected leaders of a popular revolt in the Arsenale are called to account. To everybody's surprise, the chief conspirator, Pietro Candiano, is acquitted. In a private conversation, Paolo Baglione confesses the reasons for this: he is in love with Pietro's daughter, Rosalba.

The second act is set in the courtyard of Pietro's house overlooking the Canale Grande. It is night, and the conspirators assemble to a song of 'Liberty, oh, holy Liberty'. They plan to murder Baglione prior to his marriage to the niece of the Pope. Rosalba reproaches the plotters for risking the cause of liberty for their own personal glory. She alone is willing to sacrifice her life in order to restore 'liberty, the immmortal and sacred virgin' (p. 47). To the shouts of 'Glory to you, Angel of Liberty' (p. 48) she is chosen to deliver the fatal blow to Baglione before the wedding ceremony. When everyone has gone, Rosalba receives a visit from her

---

[117] It has been published in the Italian translation of his wife, Benedetta, in Marinetti, *Teatro*, I, 3–88.

fiancée, Baldo, whom the audience recognize as Baglione disguised as a poor gondolier. He seeks to persuade her to leave the country with him, pretending that his father is opposed to their marriage. Rosalba hesitates to depart from her beloved Fatherland. Finally she agrees to go with him, but only the following day, — if she is still alive.

The third act shows the Piazzale San Marco decorated for Baglione's wedding. The people assemble (amongst them the conspirators), and a great procession of dignitaries moves into the church. When Baglione appears on a platform, Rosalba rushes up to him with a dagger hidden in a bouquet of flowers. The moment she reaches him, she recognizes in Baglione her lover Baldo and faints. Baglione seizes her and whisks her off to the Bacino, where they take a boat and leave Venice.

The last act shows the two lovers in the paradisiac surroundings of a lonely island in the Lagoon. They wait for a boat that will carry them to their chosen land of exile, Egypt. Paolo has abrogated his former life of 'vain grandeur and stupid ambition' (p. 73). In long, lyrical speeches they celebrate their love for each other. When Paolo goes to look for the boat that will take them into safety, the conspirators, led by Pietro Candiano, appear on the island. They are still implacable and intend to see their stratagem through to the end. Rosalba confesses her love for Paolo and relates that he has abandoned his service to the State and is prepared to sacrifice everything for her. Her father calls her a whore and kisses his sword which is about to put down the tyrant. When Paolo returns with the boat, the plotters attack him. Rosalba throws herself between them and is killed by her father's sword. Paolo desires only to join his dying bride on her journey to the underworld and sinks a dagger into his own heart. The conspirators fulfil the lovers' last wish: their corpses are placed in the boat and sent drifting off into the lagoon. In the background, the State ship 'Fortuna' approaches to the shouts of the sailors: 'Death to the Turks. Glory to Venice. Glory to our glorious master, Paolo Baglione.'

Marinetti's early attempt to follow the example of Victor Hugo's colourful and romantic history plays appears to have been supplemented at a later stage by incorporating d'Annunzio's poetic language into the fabric of the play. (However, La Nave cannot have exercised any influence on Paolo Baglione, because it was only written between 1905 and 1907[118]). The drama remains a fragment because it must have dawned on the author that it failed on every account to reach the standards set by the two masters he tried to emulate. The dramatic construction of the play is feeble, the lyrical interludes are heavy-handed, and the 'baroque' settings copy the worst traits of grand-opéra stage design. It was therefore wise of Marinetti to suppress this work of youth. But although its artistic merits are rather pitiable, it is interesting for the way in which Marinetti handled its political theme — the glory of the Fatherland — and the questions he raised as to who must be regarded as the best servants of the State.

---

[118] See Pietro Chiara, Vita di Gabriele d'Annunzio (Milan, 1978), pp. 162 and 187.

There is no indication that Marinetti felt any sympathy for the conspirators. The popular uprising is presented as a revolt of very dubious legitimacy. The plotters' claim to serve the ideals of liberty is rhetoric and deserves little credence. Rosalba's pride of 'not participating in [this] foul scuffle of vile and stupid prattlers' (p. 46) is believable, but there is an ironic touch in her statement that her fiancé Baldo (i. e. Baglione) 'just like me adores liberty, the immortal and sacred virgin' (p. 47). Against their overflowing rhetoric Marinetti sets the more tangible sentiments of the blind Arsenale worker Giovanni. He had been chosen to supervise the building of the 'Fortunata' and feels 'a great joy in his heart' on the day of the launch, proclaiming: 'I have caressed so much the flanks of the *Fortunata* during my ten years of work under her colossal keel. [. . .] All my life I have worked for the power and the glory of my Fatherland.' (pp. 8, 14) It is unclear whether, in the final version of the play, Marinetti intended to enlarge on this contrast of practical versus rhetoric patriotism. His pronounced and highly symbolic use of the State ship 'Fortunata' (she is seen in the first and the last act) indicates an attempt to give the theme of patriotism an allegorical treatment. Both camps in the play pretend to want the best for the State and therefore seek to protect Venice against the opposite party. The patricians regard the conspirators as vile schemers out to gain personal glory and power, whilst the rebels believe the senate to be corrupt and Baglione a tyrant. The two camps are prepared to kill each other in order to reach their respective political aims. Only the two protagonists are united in pursuing the same idealist objectives. Here, patriotic love is translated into human love, but it can only be realized in exile (and it cannot be coincidental that Paolo and Rosalba want to flee to Egypt!). But 'pure' love is denied fulfilment by the surrounding hostile forces. The two lovers reach their ideal only in death. While their dead bodies drift into the lagoon, we can see the 'Fortunata' in the background, probably to remind us that the power and glory of the Fatherland can only be achieved through a pact of all patriotic forces, from the patriciate down to the populace.

Critical writings on the theatre

To what extent *Paolo Baglione* was the immature product of a school boy and how soon Marinetti moved beyond the dramatic parameters that informed this play, becomes apparent in Marinetti's critical writings of his student years. As a collaborator on *Anthologie-Revue, La Plume, La Revue blanche, La Revue d'art dramatique*, and *La Vogue* he furnished these magazines with reviews that expressed his new aesthetic positions derived from many visits to the Teatro Lirico, La Scala, the Odeon, and the Teatro Manzoni. In the contemporary debate between *verismo* on the one hand and the poetic drama of ideas on the other, Marinetti took a clear stand in favour of the latter. When *La città morta* was premiered at the Teatro Lirico in 1901 and received a negative reception, Marinetti was 'enraged and organized a counterattack to defend Gabriele d'Annunzio, invading with hundreds of others the stalls of the theatre [. . .] delivering boxes to the ears and blows to the bellies' of the conservative spectators.[119] Similarly, in his reviews he reviled the retrograde *camorra* who tried to keep modern drama out of the Italian theatre.[120] Marinetti disapproved of the Milanese audiences, who had been raised on a diet of *pièces-bien-faites* and therefore went 'to the theatre only to laugh, digest [...] and look for an erotic *frisson* in one of these scenes with an amorous *pas-de-deux*'.[121] He not only rejected the bourgeois comedies of the period that catered for this type of audience, but also the verist plays of Praga and Rovetta because of their banal subject matter, lack of poetic language, and futile search for authenticity.[122] His opposition to scenic Naturalism was made unmistakably clear when he reviewed the production of *La città morta* by Zacconi and Duse and failed it on account of its 'exaggerated and minute realism' and vulgar banality, which in his view killed off the 'poetic splendour' of d'Annunzio's text.[123]

Instead of the Realist tradition in theatre in both its artistic and commercial guise, Marinetti opted for the drama of Poetic Idealism. Theatre, in his view, had to overcome the banality of our every-day life experience. It had to have 'a useful influence on the human soul like (and sometimes even more than) alcohol and love, by making us forget reality and instead giving us access to the world of dreams'.[124] This dream found fulfilment in the world of pure art; therefore 'a work of art counts solely because of the intensity of the dream it contains and evokes'.[125]

For this reason — and in total contrast to his later aesthetics — he was filled with 'exceeding admiration for Wagner, who stirs up the delirious heat in my blood and is such a friend of my nerves that willingly, out of love, I would lay myself down with him on a bed of clouds, so much am I enamoured with him, right down to the most hidden heart strings of my very being.'[126] But it was Wagner, the anti-traditionalist and revolutionary, the creator of musical dramas of great emotional intensity and of operas that gave expression to modernist sensibilities, who earned his praise:

---

[119] See *La grande Milano*, p. 84. The reason for the negative reaction was, as he put it in his review of the production in *La Revue blanche* (see below), 'des beautés indiscutables de haute poésie que le public normal de nos théâtres ne saurait apprécier.'

[120] See, for example, 'Une camorra Milanaise: Première et unique représentation de *Messaline*, l'opéra de M. Isidore de Lara', in *L'Art dramatique et musical* (April 1901), pp. 254–55.

[121] *L'Art dramatique et musical* (December 1901), p. 701.

[122] See, for example, the review of '*Le due Coscienze*, drame en trois actes, par Gerolamo Rovetta' in *L'Art dramatique et musical* (February 1901), pp. 122–23, where he writes: 'Ce n'est ni le théâtre nourri de pensées, audacieux et poignant de E.-A. Butti, ni le théâtre élégant, souple et spirituel de Giannino-Antona Traversi, c'est le journal quotidien d'une pipelette quelque peu cancanière [...] et vraiment l'on ne s'amuse pas assez aux inepties de M. Rovetta pour que l'on puisse supporter le jargon barbare dont il cuisine ses comédies.'

[123] 'Le Théâtre en Italie: *La Ville Morte*, tragédie de Gabriele d'Annunzio', in *La Revue blanche*, 25, no. 192 (1 June 1901), 227–28.

[124] 'Vittorio Pica', in *Anthologie-Revue* (May 1899), p. 132.

[125] 'La Resurrection de Lazarus', in *Anthologie-Revue* (September 1898), p. 239.

[126] Nothing could be further from this confession in *La grande Milano*, p. 21 than his manifesto *Down with the Tango and Parsifal* of 1914, where he denounced the 'langorous boredom' and 'musical neurasthenia' of Wagner's operas and declared that 'Wagner the innovator of fifty years ago, whom we defended when he needed it, has now been surpassed by Debussy, Strauss and by our great Futurist Pratella, and his work has therefore lost all meaning.' (TeI 84; Flint 70)

Wagner pays no regard to harmony in music, its peacefulness and logical equilibrium, its graceful flight like a dove gliding over a bed of flowers. Instead, he gives in to frenetic exuberance and rises towards the impossible. The classical line, equilibrium and sobriety have disappeared from art as order, meditation and silence have disappeared from life.[127]

Marinetti defended Wagnerian aesthetics[128] because he rated the German composer as 'the greatest decadent genius and therefore the most appropriate artist for our modern souls'.[129] Consequently, he also supported the Italian Wagnerian composer Perosi,[130] whose daring modernity represented to him the exact opposite to the 'nauseating sweetness', 'sickly mustiness', 'insupportable platitudes', and 'rancid storylines' of Puccini's operas.[131]

Marinetti's highest esteem in the dramatic field was reserved for d'Annunzio,[132] Maeterlinck[133] and Butti. The latter was a close friend of his, and judging from Marinetti's reviews of Butti's plays, the two had a great deal of aesthetic and political ideas in common. Marinetti admired Butti for his ability to shock his viewers out of their complacency and to force them to leave their routines and

---

[127] La Plume (15 February 1901), pp. 128–29. In 1902, the journal L'Ermitage published an opinion poll amongst poets, Les Poètes et leur poète, and received the following answer from Marinetti: 'I particularly like Stéphane Mallarmé because [...] he dreamt of creating a poetic symphony as definitive and magical as those executed by Richard Wagner in the field of music.' L'Ermitage, 13 (1902) 121.

[128] See 'Mascagni contre Wagner', in La Plume, no. 283 (15 February 1901), pp. 127–28 and 'Une œuvre nouvelle de Mascagni: Le Maschere', in La Revue blanche, no. 184 (1 February 1901), pp. 230–31.

[129] 'Mascagni contre Wagner', p. 128. In 'Une œuvre nouvelle de Mascagni: Le Maschere', p. 230, he describes Wagner as 'un besoin créé par la civilisation et les littératures modernes'.

[130] See the review 'La Résurrection de Lazare', in Anthologie-Revue, 1, no. 12 (September 1898), 236–39, the essay 'Lorenzo Perosi', in Anthologie-Revue, 2, no. 4 (February 1899), 73–74, and the review of 'Mose: Poème symphonique vocal', in L'Art dramatique et musical (November 1901), pp. 637–38.

[131] I cannot refrain from quoting a passage from his review of Tosca at the Teatro dal Verme: 'Une reprise absurde autant que retentissante de La Tosca, opéra de Puccini. L'exécution parfaite a mis une fois de plus en évidence la platitude insupportable de cette soi-disant musique qui fait délirer le gros public. Jamais les foires aux pains d'épice (tambours, accordéons, orgues de barbaries essoufflés) ne surpasseront le discordant brouhaha et les mélopées abrutissantes que les héros de Sardou-Illica-Giacosa glapissent sur une orchestration de nègres! On retrouve dans La Tosca tous les refrains usés, les rengaines rances des fêtes foraines, avec le relent nauséabond su sucre filé, des fritures et — surtout — la désespérante odeur de la crasse intellectuelle! Et cèst (hélas!) pour fair mousser M. Puccini, que Ricordi, le premier éditeur d'Italie, fait une guerre acharnée à tous les maestros Italiens (vieux, jeunes, célèbres et inconnus!) et ... à la musique de Richard Wagner!' L'Art dramatique et musical (November 1901), p. 636.

[132] See his essay, 'Le Théâtre de Gabriele d'Annunzio', in La Revue d'art dramatique (May 1901), pp. 420–26, where he writes: 'Je me range donc contre ses détracteurs et j'approuve a priori sa noble tentative de rénover le théâtre italien en s'inspirant aux lignes grandioses et imposantes de la tragédie grecque. [...] Je tiens à déclarer avant tout, que je considère Gabriele d'Annunzio, au théâtre comme dans le roman, le plus grand artiste italien d'aujourd'hui.' (pp. 420–421)

[133] In La grande Milano, p. 48 he reports on his evenings spent with Enrico Annibale Butti reading Maeterlinck's plays and listening to Pelléas et Mélisande. Debussy's impressionist orchestration was not at all to his liking. He would have preferred a Wagnerian composition, since he regarded the Leitmotif technique as a musical equivalent to Maeterlinck's dramaturgy of repetition. See the essays on Perosi, cited in note 130 (the one of February 1899) dedicated to Maeterlinck, and in the 1898 review he declared his particular admiration for L'Intruse, L'Interieur, and La Mort de Tintagiles). Marinetti's own use of Maeterlinckian undertones can be found in the dramatic poems contained in Destruction (see below, pp. 49–51) and the Light Plays in La Ville charnelle (see below, pp. 74–75).

habits behind. His 'audacious theses', presented as 'a mixture of dream and reality, profoundness and style', were extremely daring and perturbing to Italian audiences. His dialogues had 'the piercing beauty of a duel of souls' and made Marinetti proclaim: 'I know few thing in the theatre that are so heart-gripping'.[134] It was both their form and content that made Butti's plays 'unleash a storm of controversy, of booes and frenetic applause'.[135] Marinetti could easily identify with their decadent, individualist and anarchist heroes, and it did not astonish him that

> the high-life audience of the Teatro Manzoni went into a disappointed sulk that turned into a grimace when the anarchist entered the stage. Amongst the most hostile were the stocky bankers of Milan and all the aristocrats [...]. To them the tragedy was annoying, inoppportune, disquieting and aggressive, especially after the strikes that shook Italy, and Milan in particular, last summer. [...] It therefore did not take long before the irritation of the audience at the Manzoni turned into ferocious rage.[136]

Marinetti clearly relished the scenes that Butti's play provoked in the theatre. However, it seems typical to me that although he expressed his sympathies with the socialist and anarchist ideas proclaimed in the play, he also subscribed to the author's belief that egotism, cruelty and despotism are indelible traits of human nature, and that therefore 'it is a an absurdity to use violence and revolutions to bring about the happiness of mankind.'[137] Bearing in mind that in the previous issue of L'Art dramatique et musical the editors had announced that Marinetti was about to publish a play on 'the socialist scullery boys' (which later he turned into the outrageous drama, Le Roi Bombance[138]), we can see that Marinetti's shift into a pre-Futurist mode of thinking received considerable inspiration from Butti's drama of ideas.

However, it took Marinetti several years to turn his thèses audacieuses on the 'Holy Scullery-Boys' into a play that could be published and performed. In the meantime, he was busy producing a considerable corpus of poems. Initially, his reputation rested solely on works published in literary journals, such as Anthologie-Revue, La Vogue, La Revue blanche, La Plume, and Verde e azzurro. In 1902, the Editions de la Plume issued his first book, a cycle of nineteen poems, called La Conquête des étoiles, dedicated to his friend and mentor, Gustave Kahn. Its theme and language prefigured many concerns of the Futurist poet of 1909 and

---

[134] 'Mouvement théâtral: Drames nouveaux. Lucifero, drame en quatre actes, par E. A. Butti', in L'Art dramatique et musical (February 1901), pp. 118–21.

[135] 'Una Tempesta, tragédie moderne en cinq actes, par E.-A. Butti', in L'Art dramatique et musical (December 1901), pp. 698–701.

[136] Ibid., pp. 700–01.

[137] The two protagonists of the play were 'Adolphe, qui nous apparat aussitôt comme un humanitaire attendri, un socialiste partisan des évolutions calmes et des réformes bienfaisantes', and his anarchist companion, who tried to convince him to sell his father's lands 'non en vue d'une philanthropie directe, mais au profit exclusif et pour la propaganda de l'Idée'. Ibid., p. 699. In the end, both are living proof of the 'absurdité de la violence et des révolutions pour la conquête du bonheur collectif'. Ibid., p. 700.

[138] The brief note, placed at the end of the 'News from Italy' column in November 1901, p. 640, reads: 'M. F.-T. Marinetti, le poète et le critique italien qui écrit avec tant de goût et de talent en français, annonce un drame satirique et fantastique en quatre actes: Les Marmitons sacrés'. On Marinetti's development of the 'Scullery-Boys' theme see below, note 168.

were a first indication that some proto-Futurist tendencies had begun to take shape in Marinetti's literary output from *c.* 1900 onwards.

La Conquête des étoiles, D'Annunzio intime, and *La Momie sanglante*

The Conquest of the Stars takes as its theme the revolt of the sea against the stars. The waves challenge the stars' reign of idealism and romanticism. In a state of 'unbridled drunkenness' they want to spit into the stars' 'majestic faces'. The stars' deceptive looks, false tears and poisoned kisses have seduced many youths during 'perversely beautiful evenings' and at the end left them behind as 'petrified cadavers'. Now the 'knights of the sea' gather their forces and gallop to the battlefield. The waves send their 'infernal charge' into the sky, and heaven answers with a million bolts of lightning. Finally, the skies are overcome by the might of the 'sovereign sea', and 'the great heart of night calms down, her voluptuousness satiated, and finds a rest in the vaporous caresses of a virgin-blue and smiling dawn.'[139]

Marinetti's symbolist poetry again-and-again uses the metaphor of the Sea[140] as the Mother of Revolution (the word-play *mer-mère* is systematically exploited in the poems) and the theme of the conquest of the stars representing, like the moon, sentimentality, romanticism, and the rule of the antiquated mentality. There is a Promethean courage behind this revolt, and the Dionysian vitality of Nietzsche's *Übermensch* is clearly alluded to. The image of the sea is an emblematic representation of the life forces in their violent as well as alluring form of appearance. In some of the poems, the sea is depicted as a voluptuous lover caressing and seducing the knights with the soft rustle of her waves. But when the force of rebellion gathers momentum, she is an awesome sight to behold. However, even in her rôle as conqueror and demiurge she is described as possessing great beauty: the beauty of the wild life forces, the beauty of rebellion and war.

One of the Nietzschean 'demi-gods' was the subject of his next publication, a critical study of *Gabriele d'Annunzio intime* (Milan: Edizioni del giornale *Verde e azzurro*,[141] s. d. [1903]). D'Annunzio had become a household name in Italy, partly because of his 'disreputable' novel *Il piacere*, and partly because of his scandalous life style that flaunted traditional morality and social conventions. His well-publicized love-affair with Eleanore Duse had given rise to the plays *La città morta* (1898), *La Gioconda* (1898), *La gloria* (1899), and *Francesca da Rimini* (1902).

---

[139] Marinetti, *Scritti francesi*, p. 128.

[140] The metaphor is, of course, very common in all Symbolist poetry. Marinetti may have received some direct influence from Verhaeren. See Mariani, *Il primo Marinetti*, p. 5.

[141] The review *Verde e azzuro* was published by Marinetti's close friend, Umberto Notari who reprinted, in this issue, a number of articles that had previously appeared in the French magazine *Gil Blas*. The brochure can hardly be classified as a critical study of d'Annunzio's intimate life, for Marinetti had never met the poet. Instead of a critical assessment of d'Annunzio's life and *œuvre* he offered mere praise and flattery for his poetic hero.

FIG. 7.   Marinetti at the Kursall in Rimini

The *enfant terrible* of the literary establishment had become the idol of the young generation of Italian poets. Nearly single-handedly he had abolished the dominance of late-romantic and classicist aesthetics and established a new literary trend. His own flamboyant decadence was the best representation of the highly cultured but equally immoral heroes of his literary creations. Marinetti, too, succumbed to the spell of this colourful poet. He chose d'Annunzio as his hero and imitated his literary style in much of his poetry and early dramatic writing of this period.

FIG. 8. Marinetti on the title page of the Portuguese magazine, *O Oriente*, 1908

There are a number of d'Annunzian touches in his next work, the bizarre and mannerist fable *La Momie sanglante* (Milan: Editions du journal *Verde e azzurro*, s. d. [1904]). It is a short epithalamic *novella*, presented as a gift at the wedding of his friend Guiglielmo Anastasi. Marinetti introduces the tale by calling it 'a work impregnated with funeral aroma and pulsating with desire like a rosebush for the sun; it dares to raise Amor's goblet inlaid with stars and audaciously to toast Death during the triumphant feast of radiant youth.' (p. 133)

The story is based on an Egyptian legend[142] and is concerned with beautiful Ilaï, daughter of Pharao Bocchoris (Bekenrinef) of the 24th Dynasty. She is roused from her mortal sleep by the 'corrosive light of the Moon'. She 'burns with voluptuous anguish' and demands from the Moon, her 'sister and maid', the 'cold flesh' of her former lover, Nubar. She remembers how the Moon promised them 'the future joy of a sublime and mystical union in the blue lands of the clouds', and recalls what she has done to fulfil this aim: 'Oh Moon! It is to you that I offer the martyrdom of my heart and the sacrifice of my joy! All because you wanted my body to remain pure. It was in order to obey you, oh Moon, that I refused my beautiful and downy breasts impatient to be taken and bitten and eaten with pleasure.' (p. 136) All the details of that last 'fatal night', when they were both entombed, come back to her mind. It dawns on her that her belief in the lunar promises were ill-guided: 'Is this possible? That you are so wicked? O thousand-times accursed Moon! [...] It's you who is to blame! Infamous sorceress! [...] It's you who is a criminal!' (pp. 140–42)

The analogy of moon and false romantic sentiments that prevent lovers from satisfying their carnal desires is explored to the full in the monologue. Marinetti employs a wide spectrum of decadent and symbolist imagery, with more than an occasional bow in the direction of Baudelaire, Nerval, and Edgar Allan Poe. It mixes ingredients taken from the Orientalist and Gothic novel and creates a rather bizarre new genre: the funebral epithalamium.

Baldissone has called the novella 'una *pièce* teatrale',[143] and indeed, the setting in a crypt (with indication of décor and specification of mimics, gesture, and movement of the protagonist) explains why Marinetti later listed this monologue amongst his works as a 'poema drammatico'. What Kahn had achieved for poetry,[144] Marinetti attempted with this occasional publication for short prose pieces.

Destruction

In his next work, *Destruction* (Paris: Librairie Léon Vanier, 1904), Marinetti returned to some of the themes explored in *La Conquête des étoiles*. In fact, both were written more or less simultaneously, as transpires from an interview Marinetti gave to *Verde e azzurro* in October 1903: 'Last winter I finished *Destruction*, an erotic and anarchist poem, which will be published next month by Léon Vanier.'[145] It is the first work which Marinetti later acknowledged as being 'Futurist' (the

---

[142] It is again alluded to in the story 'Cacce arabe' in *Scatole d'amore in conserva* (Rome, 1927), and *Il fascino dell'Egitto* (Milan, 1933), p. 74. On Marinetti's Orientalism and the influence of Klingsor, Verhaeren, Kahn, and others see Mariani, *Preistoria del futurismo*, pp. 101–08.

[143] Baldissone, *Marinetti*, p. 33.

[144] On his 'samedis poétiques' see *La Revue d'art dramatique* (December 1897), pp. 1038–41; in more general terms on the new dramatic genre created and fostered by Kahn see the essay by J. F. Louis Merlet, 'Le Poème dramatique', *La Revue d'art dramatique* (June 1901), pp. 493–94.

[145] Quoted by Jannini in *Scritti francesi*, p. 24.

Italian edition of 1911 is called *Distruzione. Poema Futurista*). Its language is still firmly rooted in the Symbolist tradition, but its content is as violently anarchistic as the Futurist 'dynamite' Marinetti was later to employ in his attacks on the cultural establishment.[146]

Destruction begins with a prologue, entitled 'Invocation to the omnipotent Sea, imploring her to deliver me from the Ideal', and finishes with an epilogue, 'Invocation to the avenging Sea, begging her to deliver us from infamous reality'. The whole cycle ends with 'fanfares guerrières: Holà hé ... Holà hoo! ... Dètruisons! ... Dètruisons!' The literary forms chosen for the thirteen sections of the cycle are more varied than those in *La Conquête des étoiles*. They range from poems to poetic monologues to fully-fledged dramatic scenes. The 'divine sea' and the 'imperious stars' are again central metaphors in the work. Whilst the water represents ever-changing mobility, the stars 'lie cool ... and unyielding' in space. The sea is 'adventurous', but the stars are 'nostalgic'. Exposed to the influence of these forces are a number of human figures. At one end of the spectrum we find the 'mendicant of love', who seeks 'to nourish his dreams with love and kisses' and therefore 'lusts for the sky's jewels' and her 'tragic splendour'.[147] At the other extreme we are presented with a wild and cheerful 'puerile soul', who shuns the 'lethargic stars' and instead seeks to quench his thirst 'with the freshness of [the sea's] spray' and revels in 'a triumphant orgy of the senses' (p. 151).

Section five is a semi-dramatic piece for three voices, *Nocturne*. A young couple spend a romantic evening by the sea, pining for each other and exchanging kisses 'impregnated with ideals' (p. 168). With 'pale faces' they observe the stars ('This golden but accursed city', p. 173, that lies 'far away from our lips' and 'can never be reached', p. 169). The Sea comments on this scene by comparing the couple to two blind men wandering in a labyrinth and to two deaf people imprisoned in a dungeon.

The Woman is less spiritual in her desires than her lover and gets restless with his 'squandering his desires on the chimeric pupilles of the stars' (p. 169). Her carnality is aroused by the voice of the Sea, whom the man therefore calls 'an accursed sorceress' (p. 171). The Sea warns them: 'Your kisses will never be anything but an illusion, because the whole of the infinite sky will always keep you apart.' (p. 172) In her final speech, the Sea compares the man to a wanderer lost in the Milky Way,

---

[146] It is interesting to note that Canto XIII (*Invocation ... contre les villes*) was renamed *Eloge de la dynamite*, when it appeared in *Poesia* II, 6–8 (July–September 1906), and *Aux Révolutionnaires russes*, when it was printed in *La vita letteraria* III, 2 (16 January 1906). The 'Russian revolutionaries' are, of course the anarchists, for whom he continued to have the greatest admiration: 'Some anarchists disguised as coffin-bearers solemnly carry into the imperial palace a hearse full of bombs, and the Czar is blown up with all his obstinate medievalism, like the cork in a last bottle of over-aged champagne.' *Guerra, sola igiene*, TeI 276 (Flint 106–07).

[147] Many of Marinetti's metaphors seem to have received inspiration from Nietzsche's *Thus Spake Zarathustra*. Compare, for example, the *Chanson du mendiant d'amour* with the following passage: 'From the high drippeth the star and the gracious spittle, and for the high longeth every starless bosom. The moon has its court and the court its moon-calves; unto all, however, that cometh from the court do the mendicant people pray.' Book III, ch. 51 (On Passing-By).

wasting his energy by travelling from star to star in search of his Ideal, but never reaching the height of the sky to find fulfilment.

The Maeterlinckian tone of this piece is repeated in another semi-dramatic poem. Canto 9 is a *Song of Jealousy* for two voices. A lover visits his girl friend, who has fallen asleep on the beach and is dreaming of the Sea, her 'obscene Goddess'. When he awakens her, she gives her enticing, nude body not to him, but to the waves of the Sea. The lyrical duologues are interrupted by descriptive sections written in the same poetic style and reflecting the thoughts of the male protagonist.

The most dramatic piece is section 8, *Dans les cafés de nuit.*[148] It begins with a poem in which the author remembers his adolescent days in Egypt. He spent whole evenings looking at the stars and the moon, until he began to resent the lugubrious atmosphere produced by the 'grand, accursed Dream' (p. 222). So he decided 'to strangle his Dream in some place, a crossroad of a busy street, or a brothel, or — better still — a *café-concert*' (p. 222). The plot of the play begins in one of these 'night cafés, where one kills one's Dream'. 'I', that is: Marinetti, sits at a table with 'My Soul', waiting for Joy to arrive. The electric lights have dispersed 'the acidic and corrosive nights of full moon' (p. 224). The Soul expects a 'woman with devouring blue eyes, whom I love and have longed for since I have felt the hope of life, the hunger for love and pleasure. She is the darling, who has been promised to me by the Stars.' (p. 225) Until now, the Soul has been waiting in vain for this great ideal of a 'blossoming woman with lips of perfume' to materialize.

While 'I' and 'My Soul' are drinking in the Café, Loulou arrives, 'her mouth shaped like a heart, her eyes radiating sensuality' (p. 229). She is the Soul's lover and has been the object of many of his poems. Some friends, who have read the poems dedicated to Loulou, enter and declare that these works are of poor quality. The Soul is indignant about their lack of taste and appreciation and proclaims that they do not understand anything about art and poetry.

At this point, 'I' gives 'My Soul' a lengthy piece of advice: he is talented, maybe even a genius; but it is foolish of him to aspire to 'the unreachable Absolute'. He may be satisfied with the ecstasy of having created pure beauty. But what good does it do him? I's advice is: 'Boldly spit on life, on glory, on women, on love [. . .]. Art is unreachable like the stars; and it is sad, so very sad to worship the stars [. . .]. Doesn't one invariably end up mid-way on the calvary road to impossible artistic perfection' (p. 231)? With regard to Loulou this means: stop idealizing and worshipping her with your poetry. Become aware that she is a real woman, who desires more than poetic effusions. She loves you as you love her. Why not enjoy her caresses and take 'this sweet young woman with spring lips to a warm, locked room, watch her slowly undress', and then enjoy her *body* in 'a great protective bed that absolves every remorse' (p. 232)?

[148] It has been translated by Martinelli as *Lulu* in *Theatre Three*, no. 2 (Spring 1987), pp. 53–58.

Loulou agrees and invites the Soul: 'Tonight, you'll come to my place, and I will cure you.' (p. 233). The play ends with the report: 'I accompanied them to her house. On the threshold, my Soul, shakily, saluted me with a slight, triumphant smile. Because, deep down, you know, my Soul is a very beastly creature.' (p. 233)

In the Night Cafés is a particularly interesting piece, because it documents the impact Paris had on Marinetti's artistic development. He not only discovered the literary world of Symbolism, but also a new type of popular entertainment — *café-concert* and Music-hall — which he began to regard as an expression of modern collective sensibilities. Loulou is a representative of this world: she does not want to be, as women were in the past, an object of romantic serenades. She wants to be recognized as a physical being, which is exactly what happens in these night cafés: 'Music-hall [...] snatches every veil from woman, all the phrases, all the sighs, all the romantic sobs that mask and deform her, and — instead — brings out her marvellous animal qualities'.[149] The atmosphere of electric lights and gay, modern music is the opposite of the hypnotizing *clairs de lune* and the 'bitter nostalgic taste' of old-fashioned orchestras (p. 226). Later, in the *Variety Theatre Manifesto* of 1913, Marinetti was to express the idea thus:

> Music-hall systematically disparages ideal love and its romantic obsession that repeats the nostalgic languors of passion to satiety [...]. It lowers lust to the natural function of coitus, deprives it of every mystery, every crippling anxiety, every unhealthy idealism. [...] Café-concert performances in the open air on the terraces of casinos offer an amusing battle between an agonising clair de lune, tormented by infinite desperations, and the electric light [...] Naturally, the electric light triumphs and the soft, decadent clair de lune is defeated.[150]

In the surroundings of the café-concert, Loulou — who until now has been the, unfulfilled, promise of the stars — becomes flesh and blood. Her idealized image is stripped of its romantic trappings. As a real human being she is united with the Soul. *Physis* and *psyche* become one. The end of the piece implies that their union will produce the new race of the future, where the old dichotomies of body and intellect, art and life, are overcome.

It is interesting to note that the same artistic programme can be found in another Lulu play of the period, Wedekind's *Die Büchse der Pandora*. The theme of a future life, where the spirit and flesh will be joined in a harmonious union, had already been explored by the author in *Frühlings Erwachen* (1890–91, first produced 1906 in Berlin). During his visit to Paris in 1891, Wedekind was a regular attender at music-hall, café-concert, and circus performances. His new artistic credo combined the erotic concerns of his earlier play with the new dramatic formats to be found in popular theatre. The result was his first Lulu-play, based on Félicien Champsaur's

[149] *Variety Theatre Manifesto*, TeI 72 (Flint 118).
[150] TeI 74 (Flint 119).

Lulu. Pantomime en un acte.[151] There is no evidence that Marinetti possessed any detailed information of the Leipzig première of *Der Erdgeist* (1898) or that he read the first printed edition of the play (1895) and the subsequent *Die Büchse der Pandora* (1902). It is more likely that Marinetti received inspiration for his own Loulou play, *In the Night Cafés*, from personal experiences in Parisian music-halls. He may, however, have taken the name of the character from Champsaur's popular and well-known pantomime,[152] but again there is no evidence that he actually saw or read the play.

Another canto whose proto-Futurist quality merits mentioning is *Le Démon de la vitesse* (The Demon of Speed). Parts of it were published separately with the titles *La Folie des tramways* and *Chant futuriste*.[153] The first section of the canto is dedicated to Gustave Kahn, who in 1901 had published his eulogy to modern life, *L'Esthétique de la rue*.[154] This ten-part poem of epic scope and dramatic verve describes with highly evocative power a mad journey into death.

After having spent a languid night with his lover on the 'Terraces of Love', the hero 'regretfully leaves the sleeping port' (p. 185) and begins a journey 'that leads towards appealing liberty' (p. 186). He steps onto a train which is variably described as 'fantastique' (p. 186), 'hallucinant', 'frénétique' (p. 187), 'chimérique' (p. 188), etc. The hero's heart is gripped by the 'madness' and 'miracle' of its 'aggressive pace' (p. 187). This 'diabolic serpent' (p. 188) 'reverberates with a song of demons' (p. 187), and like 'an apocalyptic torrent' (p. 188) it sweeps him away to his destiny, which is 'as incalculable as the abyss' (p. 189).

He passes through a city with one-hundred-thousand-year old houses. They are 'decrepit', 'lugubrious' and have 'mummified façades' (p. 189). They declare him mad and his journey 'an absurd flight [...] of a suicidal dream' (p. 189). But he does not let himself be stopped and continues his race 'beyond the confines of space and time' (p. 191). In the fourth part, the train 'dances amidst the whirl of a desert storm' (p. 192). It 'soars up and forges ahead into the liberating and despotic Evening' (p. 192). He reaches a port, and 'the artificial splendour [...] of this enclosed sea' (p. 193) invites him to rest. But he does not give in to the temptation,

[151] See Artur Kutscher, 'Eine unbekannte französische Quelle zu Frank Wedekinds "Erdgeist" und "Büchse der Pandora"', in *Das Goldene Tor*, 2 (1947), 497–505. On Wedekind's erotic philosophy see Alfons Höger, *Hetärismus und bürgerliche Gesellschaft im Frühwerk Frank Wedekinds*, Munich 1981; Thomas Medicus, *Die große Liebe: Ökonomie und die Konstruktion der Körper im Werk von Frank Wedekind*, Marburg 1982; Josephine Schröder Zebralla, *Wedekinds religiöser Sensualismus*, Frankfurt/M. 1986. On Wedekind and Parisian music-hall see his diary, Frank Wedekind, *Die Tagebücher: Ein erotisches Leben*, ed. by G. Hay (Frankfurt/M. 1986) (English edition: *Diary of an Erotic Life* [Oxford, 1990]) and Laurence Senelick, 'Wedekind and Music Hall', in *New Theatre Quarterly*, 4 (1988), 326–39.
[152] There were many editions and also a novel, *Lulu: Roman clownesque* (Paris, 1900).
[153] The first appeared in *La Rénovation esthétique*, no. 2 (July 1906), the second in *Poesia*, vol. 5, nos 3–6 (April–July 1909). The latter was also included in *Poeti futuristi* (Milan: Edizioni futuriste di 'Poesia', 1912).
[154] This three-hundred-page study was inspired by Romains' Unanimism and described the new form of street life that had developed since the Second Empire, centred on boulevards, cafés and music-halls. He analysed Haussmann's urbanization, the new façades and ornaments of houses, the multi-coloured posters and the newly installed gas lights as a 'décor', a stage set for modern street life.

nor to that of some women; because what good does it do 'to enquire after the leaven of their flesh and their breasts annointed with spices, since now my soul can enjoy but little their embraces' (p. 194).[155] He continues his journey through 'the vindicative forests' (p. 195) and spurs on his train: 'Be mad, fiery train of my soul, be as mad as you wish, the madder the better! Answer them with bursts of white and steamy laughter, with your clear whistling crowned with horror. — Poor wisdom! Oh joy to feel absurd!' (p. 195) The train again gathers momentum, and he rejoices: 'What ecstasy! [...] What rapture!' (p. 196) The skies are deafened by his 'giant steps', and they send the 'taming elements' to seize his reins. With their 'enormous strangulating pincers they enclose [his] vagabonding heart' (p. 196), but he receives the support of the Wind, whose arms pull him towards the Infinite. So the triumphant course of the train continues. There is 'no delay, no slackening of the reins. [...] Faster, faster again. Let the pulse of the machine increase its élan a hundredfold! — Here comes my train rebounding in a halo of flames and bleeding gold!' (p. 198)

In part 6 he finds himself amidst a Sabbath of Titans and surrounded by monsters and skeletons, Erinyes and Chimeras. He sees their forges and 'tragic factories' (p. 200) and has no wish 'to visit this dormant city, wrapped up in silence, like a mummy under the pestering yoke of the stars' (p. 201). He flees the 'crucified city' (p. 201) and drives through an immense landscape. He reaches a 'sleeping city' by a 'tyrannic river' and drives into a 'grand and sombre hall of a cavernous station' (p. 203), where his train comes to a halt. Parts 7 and 8 describe his sojourn and the rest he finds in the arms of a woman, who makes him remember the night on the Terraces of Love prior to his departure.[156] They celebrate 'an impossible feast on a bed of delicate roses' (p. 207), but this cannot satisfy his 'thirst for space and the impossible [...] Josie, Josie, your arms can never enchain this heart that is longing to merge its madness with the dazzling folly of the stars.' (p. 206) Although he feels inclined to savour the moments of nostalgic love a little longer, he pulls himself away: 'Nothing must stop you, despite your immense chagrin and your enormous fatigue. There is no oasis to be found on the earth for your thirst. [...] With what could you quench your immemorial thirst?' (p. 212)

So he takes to the road again, despite his 'dancing and frenetic agony' (p. 214). An 'affectionate demon' announces his death to him. But he does not let himself be intimidated. Despite 'the tenebrous shiver of a funereal embrace that fills [his] bones and jaws' (p. 215) he exclaims: 'How could I slow down my pace and the powerful rhythm of my heart?' (p. 215) He sees in front of him 'the fearsome

---

[155] Again, there are startling similarities to Zarathustra's travels and his rest on the Happy Islands: 'Verily, with insiduous beauty do sea and life surround me and gaze upon me. O afternoon of my life! O happiness before eventide! O haven upon high seas! O peace in uncertainty. How do I mistrust all of you! Verily, distrustful I am of your insiduous beauty! Like the lover I am who distrusteth an all-too sleek smiling. [...] Away with thee, thou blissful hour! Thou broughtst me bliss without my wish; at the wrong time hast thou come. [...] There, already approacheth eventide: the sun sinketh. Away — my happiness!' Book III, ch. 47 (Involuntary Bliss).

[156] The two poems are dedicated to Mme Kahn and 'Térésah', i. e. Marinetti's girlfriend, the poetess Teresa Corinna Ubertis.

hangars' (p. 215) of death, but like a 'caught fish' he 'rebels, undefeated' (p. 216). Then the 'ice-cold breath of Death' (p. 216) brushes against him. There is a loud crash. He hears the rustling of chains and hinges: the train has been laid in fetters.

As a 'condemned sailor' (p. 217) the hero enters the city of death. His flesh is torn from his body. He is 'surrounded by the masses who envelop [him] with their tentacles' (p. 217). He is taken to 'the fateful port' (p. 218). A boat is waiting for him at the mooring. The people gather 'to savour the sublime spectacle of [his] death' (p. 219). He is ready 'to enjoy the glorious feast which Death, [his] master, will prepare in the Realm of Nothingness' (p. 220). He looks at the sea and 'contemplates the depth of the abyss through the elastic crystal of the waters' (p. 221). He breathes in 'the evocative perfume of the Paradise Lost. [His] tattered body drinks [Death's] deifying strength, and he dies, without coming to an end!' (p. 221).[157]

This anarchical and nihilistic *tour de force* is one of the most impressive achievements in Marinetti's early poetic *œuvre* and offers a good indication of the ideological foundations, on which Futurism was erected. The so-called 'machine-cult' that finds expression in the poem is not a mere fixation on technological advances, but a metaphor for a Bergsonian *élan vital*, for an exuberant life force that breaks through all barriers. The final message appears to be: better a short life of exultation that ends in early death than a slow and long existence, where all human potential lies dormant.[158]

Destruction ends with what has been promised earlier on in the cycle: *folie* and *ivresse* aroused by the *vents frénétiques* and *le chant fiévreux des mers* reach a climax of *delire, pour y trouver l'immense Oubli* (the drunken madness aroused by the frenetic winds and the feverish song of the sea reach a delirious climax in which one finds oblivion).[159] Riding on the Sea, a Black Knight appears and rings in the Apocalypse with his 'gallop of devastating cyclones'. He charges against the Sun, the 'Supreme Dream, the Star of Stars'. The 'final pandemonium of a feast of giants' begins, where everything is hurled into an abyss to the cries of 'Death is a gay mistress'. After the triumph of total destruction begins the task of 'rebuilding the legendary structures of a Great Ideal World on the ruins the Old'. This must be carried out by a new race, for 'man cannot create buildings other than prisons nor forge instruments other than chains'.

The world view expressed in *Destruction* offers an illuminating explanation of why Marinetti could only conceive of a Future that was based on the ruins of the past. The act of destruction is a celebration of the creative potential of human beings. Death is a positive 'life' force. It gives energy and dynamism to the universe. Only through death are things transformed into something new. It works as a fuel

---

[157] On the Nietzschean undertones in this end see below, pp. 70–71. Marinetti might have received direct inspiration from Nietzsche's poem *Die Sonne sinkt* (The Sun Sinks) in the *Dionysos-Dithyrambs*.
[158] Later on, in a Futurist declaration of 1910, he put it into the following words: 'Better a splendid disaster than the monotony of a daily repeated journey.' 'Rapporto sulla vittoria del Futurismo a Triste', in: Aldo Palazzeschi, *L'Incendiario* (Milan, 1910), p. 14.
[159] *La Chanson du mendiant d'Amour*, in *Scritti francesi*, pp. 173–80.

in the metamorphoses of the cosmos. As an artist and anarchist, Marinetti lent his support to this process by casting into the world a poetic grenade which seemed to be inspired by a passage in Nietzsche's *Gay Science*: 'The desire to destroy, to change, to create something new, can be expression of an exuberant force, pregnant with Future. My term for this is, as everyone knows, "Dionysian"'.[160]

Destruction was Marinetti's 'impatient dynamite: This is a gay manner of fertilizing the earth! Because the Earth, believe me, will soon be pregnant. She will grow big — until she bursts! — From a sublime star to illuminating explosions.' (p. 266) *Destruction* was conceived as an anarchical hymn to these *explosions illuminantes*. It was a poetic bombshell, which caused Baldissone to comment: 'After this 'Mer Vengeresse' follows nothing but the deluge, or rather, *après moi, le futurisme*'.[161]

The journal *Poesia*

Before Marinetti could give birth to Futurism, he had a few years in which to extend his literary experience and gather around him a number of like-minded souls with whom he could lay the foundations for this new artistic movement. An important aid to this enterprise was the launching, in 1905, of the journal *Poesia*. Initially run in conjunction with the playwright Sem Benelli and the poet Vitaliano Ponti, the organization soon rested in the hands of Marinetti alone. His flat in Via Senato 2 was the editorial office, he provided the finances, and from issue 8 of September 1906 onwards he functioned as sole editor and publisher.

Poesia could easily be compared in importance to the journals of the Florentine Movement, *Leonardo* (1903–07)and *La Voce* (1908–16). But whilst these were distinctly *Italian* in outlook, Marinetti's creation was conceived as an *international* magazine of poetry. He sought to bring about a renaissance in Italian literature by introducing the latest trends in European writing to the dormant and provincial literary scene in his home country. The main emphasis of *Poesia* was on France, but it also published new works from Germany, England, America, Russia, Scandinavia, and Spain. It certainly was not an outlet for a narrow spectrum of Milanese intellectuals and artists. The programme was neatly emblematized in the cover drawing of Alberto Martini: the poetic muse stands on a rock in the middle of the thundering sea, surrounded by the stars. Her arrow has killed an octopus, whose tentacles are extended towards Mount Parnassus. The theme and style of the drawing seems to reflect the last canto of *La Conquête des étoiles*, but here it is the force of poetry which delivers us from the suffocating tentacles of infamous reality.

The magazine not only published poetic creations that expressed an attitude of revolt against literary and social convention; it also initiated debates on new and

---

[160] *Fröhliche Wissenschaft*, § 370.
[161] Baldissone, *F. T. Marinetti*, p. 43.

FIG. 9.   Alberto Martini, Drawing of 1905 for the cover of *Poesia*, here used for the first
Futurist issue of April–July 1909

modern forms of expression (e. g. the 'enquête sur le vers libre'), the popularization
of literature (e. g. the campaign for a popular election to an Italian Academy), and
the need to update social rôle models (e. g. the referendum on the beauty of Italian
women). Marinetti also sought to introduce to the Italian public specimens of new
dramatic writing. Apart from his own *drames de lumières*, which later appeared in
La Ville charnelle, he published Gian Pietro Lucini's *Monologue de Brighella*,
Enrico Fondi's 'poème dramatique' *La Berceuse de L'Etera*, fragments from
Richard Dehmel's *Le Réveil du seigneur* and Gabriele d'Annunzio's *La Nave*, and
extracts from Enrico Corradini's *Charlotte Corday*, Nello Puccioni's *Lucrèce
Borgia*, Ricciotto Canudo's *La Mort d'Hercule*, and Enrico Cavacchioli's *Les
Corsaires*. Marinetti's commitment to the *esprit du théâtre moderne* was mainly
directed at the late-Symbolist lyrical drama of ideas; but he also lent enthusiastic
support to Alfred Jarry, whose one-act pastorale, *L'Objet aimé*, was printed along

ANNO SESTO   ANNO SESTO

POESIA

MOTORE DEL FUTURISMO

Direttore F. T. MARINETTI

ha pubblicato versi inediti dei maggiori poeti contemporanei:

MISTRAL, PAUL ADAM, HENRI DE RÉGNIER, CATULLE MENDÈS, GUSTAVE
KAHN, VIELÉ-GRIFFIN, VERHAEREN, FRANCIS JAMMES, MAUCLAIR,
JULES BOIS, STUART MERRILL, PAUL FORT, LA COMTESSE DE NOAILLES,
JANE CATULLE MENDÈS, RACHILDE, HÉLÈNE PICARD, H. VACARESCO, ecc.

G. D'ANNUNZIO, PASCOLI, MARRADI, BRACCO, BUTTI, COLAUTTI,
D. ANGELI, SILVIO BENCO, ELDA GIANELLI, A. BACCELLI, ADA NEGRI
G. P. LUCINI, D. TUMIATI, G. LIPPARINI, CAVACCHIOLI, PAOLO BUZZI,
CORRADO GOVONI, A. PALAZZESCHI, LIBERO ALTOMARE, G. CARRIERI.

SWINBURNE, SYMONS, YEATS, FRED. BOWLES, DOUGLAS GOLDRING,
SMARA, ALEXANDRE MACEDONSKI, DEHMEL, ARNO HOLZ, VALÈRE
BRUSSOV, SALVADOR RUEDA, E. MARQUINA, E. GONZALES-BIANCO,
SANTIAGO ARGUËLLO, ecc.

ABBONAMENTO ANNUO: in Italia L. 10 - all'Estero L. 15

Ogni numero, in Italia L. 1

FIG. 10.   Advertisement of 1911 for *Poesia*, now elevated to the status of 'Motor of
Futurism'

with two *poèmes en prose*. After Jarry's death Marinetti even announced that he had acquired the exclusive rights to publish Jarry's unedited works in Italy.[162]

From 1907 onwards, *Poesia* extended its activities by operating as a publishing house. Under the imprint of 'Edizioni di Poesia' it published a large number of creative and critical texts, thereby creating a 'stable' of authors, who later lent their support to Marinetti when he founded the Futurist movement.

After the death of his father, in 1907, Marinetti became a rich man. He now had the funds to pay very generous royalties to the contributors of his magazine (e. g. 100 Lire to Pascoli for an unpublished poem), and to offer well-endowed literary prizes (1000 Lire) to the winners of his poetry competitions. *Poesia* served as a base for Marinetti's wide-reaching activities as a 'cultural manager' and entrepreneur. He developed all the qualities that later gave him the reputation of being the 'caffeine of Europe'[163] (at that time he was called 'Poeta Pink' after a popular medicine). In 1906, his face began to turn up in popular caricatures — a clear indication that he was becoming a well-known character on the Italian cultural scene. He had his first biography published (Tullio Pànteo's *Il poeta Marinetti*, which was seen by many as a sign of 'impudent careerism and intolerable exhibitionism'[164]). As if this was not enough, he conducted extensive advertising campaigns and introduced American-style publicity methods to the literary establishment by sending out Christmas cakes in gratuity boxes wrapped-up in the headed paper of *Poesia*![165] In this respect Marinetti was probably right when, after 1909, he baptized *Poesia* 'Motore del Futurismo' and declared that the foundation of *Poesia* was also 'the birth of Futurism'.[166]

Le Roi Bombance

In September 1905, Marinetti published his first play, *Le Roi Bombance. Tragédie satirique en 4 actes, en prose* (Paris: Société du Mercure de France).[167] Its original title — as we have seen above — had been *Les Marmitons sacrés* (The Holy Scullery-Boys). But to avoid comparison with a work by Max Jacob, *Roi Kabul et le marmiton Gauvin*, which had appeared in Paris in 1904, the title was changed to

[162] See *Poesia*, 4, nos 11–12 (December 1908–January 1909), p. 24.
[163] See Tel 506.
[164] See Vaccari, *Vita e tumulti*, p. 185. The fact that nearly the entire book had been written by Marinetti himself has been mentioned above, note 1. A more serious indication of Marinetti's growing international fame was the publication of a special issue dedicated to 'F. T. Marinetti, Autor do ROI BOMBANCE' of the Portuguese Magazine *O Oriente* of 15 March 1908.
[165] See Salaris, *Marinetti*, p. 66.
[166] See *Marinetti e il Futurismo*, in Tel 506.
[167] The first Italian translation, by Marinetti's secretary Decio Cinti, appeared under the title *Re Baldoria. Tragedia satirica in 4 atti, in prosa* (Milan: Fratelli Treves editori (1910), 2nd edn 1920). It has been reprinted in Marinetti, *Teatro*, vol. 1. Since this is the most easily available version of the play, all my quotations will refer to this edition. On the first production in Paris, in 1909, see below, pp. 87–91. The first Italian production took place in Rome in 1929 (see the reviews in Giovanni Antonucci, *Cronache del teatro futurista* (Rome, 1975), pp. 263–71).

Roi Bombance (King Revelry).[168] This, of course, was an open invitation to associate the play with Jarry's *Ubu Roi*, which had undoubtedly served as a model and whose parentage Marinetti was apparently happy to acknowledge.[169]

The action of the play takes place in a fairy-tale kingdom, called Bourdes (French for blunder or bloomer; in the Italian edition it is populated with *citrulli*, or blockheads). The first act is set in the park of the Castle of Abundance, where King Bombance reigns. A revolution has been planned by the three Scullery-Boys, Syphon, Torte and Béchamel, supported by Estomacreux (Big-Guts) and the hungry masses of the kingdom. The Scullery-Boys promise Big-Guts the position of Superintendent of the Kitchens in exchange for his support in the conspiracy, and the Hungry-Ones are assured that they will be liberated from the spectre of Saint Putrefaction and the Ponds of the Past that surround the castle.

The Scullery-Boys approach King Bombance in their capacity as ambassadors of the Hungry-Ones. They offer the prospect of stifling the revolt, should the monarch be willing to hand over the royal kitchen to them. The King agrees, providing the three Boys prepare a banquet that will feed the starving masses.

In the second act, the three 'Cooks of Universal Happiness' have failed to fulfil their promise. The Hungry-Ones, stirred up by Estomacreux, stand outside the castle and are about to storm the seat of government while the Scullery-Boys are feasting in the cellars. The three Cooks manage to ward off the masses with the promise of a big feast, at which 20,000 calves will be cooked for them. A much-thinner looking King tells the people to what extent the government, including the three Cooks of Universal Happiness, have been starved. He wins the sympathies of the masses, who celebrate him as 'the good but most unhappy King, whose heart was always too noble and generous' (p. 65). The Court Poet confronts the people and reveals his plan of how to escape the great hunger: return to 'the land of Azure Dreams, where [...] one lives on sweet music and caressing words veiled in a hazy *clair de lune*. Beauty! Hope! Ideals! Golden Stars!' (p. 69) While the tumultuous rebels try to get rid of the poet, he declares that what they need is not meat and bread, but the 'tender Stars made of honey and gold' (p. 71). Suddenly, sunlight breaks through the sky and illuminates the Idiot (as the poet is called in the play). It is at this mystical moment that he declares himself 'the Elect of Destiny' (p. 77), who has come from the Manor of the Impossible. There, he has been

---

[168] On the cover of *La Conquête des étoiles* (1902) the play was announced under this title as being in preparation. It was completed in 1903 and accepted for publication, with a preface by Laurent Tailhade, by the Mercure de France. In *La Momie sanglante* (1904) it was announced as being in the press. Lista, *La Scène futuriste*, p. 35 quotes a letter of December 1904, where Marinetti speaks of having received the proofs of his play *Les Marmitons sacrés*. The January 1905 issue of *Poesia* announced the work, however, as *Le Roi Bombance*, with the subtitle *Les Marmitons sacrés*. When the book was finally printed, the subtitle had been withdrawn, but the first act carried the same heading.

[169] As has been mentioned above, Marinetti was a good friend of Jarry and sent him a copy of the play shortly after its appearance. The similarities between both plays were pointed out by many reviewers of the first production in Paris (see below), but as far as the figure of King Bombance is concerned, he is quite the opposite of King Ubu. Ubu is an active leader, who determines the entire plot, whilst Bombance is a inefficient glutton, unable to guide his people and to take any initiative in the government of his realm.

blessed with a kiss from 'the restorative lips of the Intangible' (p. 77) and given the shape of a terrestial Alter-Ego, in order to deliver a message of magic to the humans. For a while, the Hungry-Ones listen to his poetic sermon, but then they grow tired of his messianic tirades and hit him with their frying pans.

The Scullery-Boys enter and declare that the big meal will soon be served. The King gets so excited at the prospect that he swoons and dies. Estomacreux mourns his death and declares that the King had always been on their side and had nothing in common with the government of the three Cooks of Universal Happiness. Syphon refutes this and promises to pickle the King and keep his body as preserved meat for a future occasion. But as for the present, there will be plenty of food for everybody.

The third act describes 'The Orgy' in the interior of the Castle. The hungry masses have forced the Scullery-Boys to fulfil their promise of socializing the means of culinary production. In the general melée of the collective feast a fight breaks out over the food. Some revellers are stabbed to death, but before worse can happen, the crowning event of the feast is announced: in steaming, golden bathtubs formed like sarcophagi the roasted and stuffed King together with his courtiers are brought into the hall. While the Hungry-Ones devour the sweet aristocratic morsels, the Scullery-Boys sneak into the kitchen, where they have hidden much tastier delicacies. But Estomacreux discovers them and has them brought into the refectory, tied up like salami.

Suddenly, accompanied by thunder and lightning, an allegorical figure of the pilgrim Alkaman appears in the hall. He asks for food and joins the revellers, relating to them the story of Saint Putrefaction, the Moon Goddess and mother of King Bombance. He announces that she has risen from the Ponds of the Past and is approaching the castle with her monstrous army of beetles, frogs, and scorpions. On hearing this news, the Scullery-Boys are seized with shock and horror and die. The other revellers are overcome with nausea caused by the human flesh they have eaten. They feel they are suffocating and open the window to the hall.

This is the moment Saint Putrefaction has been waiting for. She enters the hall through the window and inspects the half-dead bodies writhing on the floor. She stops in front of Estomacreux and talks to King Bombance, who is resting — still undigested — in the rebel leader's stomach: 'Console yourself. My fiery and suffocating breath will shortly give life to a whole brood of kings, vicious and carnivorous like you were. This is the divine law: decomposing in an illusionary death in order to be reconstituted and born again in an identical shape. This is the law of decomposition that governs the world.' (pp. 180–81)

The fourth act takes place the next morning. The Hungry-Ones are still resting at the table, but by now they are double the size that they were before the Orgy. Inside their stomachs, still undigested, are the King, his counsellors, and courtiers, tormenting the cannibals who have devoured them. In between the belching and grunting noises of the Hungry-Ones we hear the King crying for help. Estomacreux tries to drown him by drinking a gallon of wine, but this only increases the pain in his stomach. Finally, the nausea makes him vomit up the King. Bombance goes and pulls out the other courtiers from the stomachs of the Hungry-Ones and orders the release of the three Scullery-Boys from their intestinal prison, so that they can stand trial for their treachery.

A courtroom is hastily set up, but before the trial begins, the Scullery-Boys manage to bribe the King and his hungry entourage by revealing a place to them, where the finest delicacies in the castle are hidden. Platters overflowing with meat are brought in and the King absolves the Boys and releases them from their chains. By now, the Hungry-Ones have recovered from their drunken state and return from the Ponds of the Past, where they had been dumped. Estomacreux bursts through the window (just as Saint Putrefaction had done in Act III), and his hordes fill the hall, searching for the King and his courtiers, who have taken shelter behind a barricade of pots and pans. Saint Putrefaction hovers over their heads, waiting to issue forth her 'vivifying and destructive breath of metempsychosis' (p. 238). Estomacreux offers his help in this process of soul migration and sets about to devour the King for a second time.

Here, the Poet intervenes again and seeks to illuminate Estomacreux on the true nature of freedom. He thinks that liberty can never be fully achieved. The quest for freedom is like a never-ending ascent to the Heights of the Absolute. Liberty cannot be an automatic consequence of abolishing the monarchy and the existing laws. The old order will only be replaced with a new one. The Hungry-Ones may dream of 'Good-natured Anarchy. This is nothing but a dream caused by almighty digestion, tiredness and nausea. Liberty? It is impossible to grasp, because it possesses an elastic amplitude that grows in direct proportion to the growth of your desires.' (p. 240) Furious about having their dreams shattered, the Hungry-Ones charge forward to kill the Poet. But he seizes the State sword from the King and kills Estomacreux and a whole row of Hungry-Ones. Then he demonstrates the ultimate act of gaining freedom: 'I have thirst for poetry [. ..]. I dream of singing the sublime song of death.' (p. 242) He takes the sword and drives it through his forehead.

The Hungry-Ones are not impressed by this heroic suicide. They search for the King to the shouts of 'Let Justice, Equality and Liberty finally reign in all stomachs and intestines!' Saint Putrefaction comments on their actions by pointing out the eternal cycle of 'Creation, Destructon, Regeneration' (p. 247). She summons her child, the vampire Ptiokaroum, who recites the lesson of the 'eternal road of thirst and hunger' (p. 248). Saint Putrefaction judges that the poet has arrived at an understanding of the laws that govern the world. Inspired by the 'Astral fire' and driven by the 'eternal hunger for the impossible happiness', he 'strove towards the Infinite, where time and space lose their names' (p. 251). Estomacreux, on the other hand, is compared to Don Quixote. His quest for justice, liberty, and equality is like fighting with 'the windmills of the Impossible' (p. 251). But nevertheless, his energy is commendable, and she encourages him: 'Draw your blue sword of hope and slice the astral meat on the celestial table and prepare for the Feast of all Feasts for all Hungry-Ones.' (p. 252) As the starving masses throw themselves onto the King and his courtiers, Ptiokaroum comments that neither now nor in the future will they be any wiser; 'they will only develop their jaws and devour each other with increasing

agility' (p. 252). Saint Putrefaction agrees: eating the King 'will not calm your
hunger. It will not give you an ounce of happiness. Happiness is to be found
elsewhere. (She makes a wide gesture towards the horizon)' (p. 253). She asks
Ptiokaroum, if he wants to eat the Poet's 'white brain impregnated with azure'
(p. 253), but he declines. He finds it as repulsive as that of the others, and he already
has indigestion. Saint Putrefaction opens his beak and forces him to vomit. The
play ends with a torrent of blood running out of his mouth and inundating the
stage.

   This verbose and scenically-challenging monstrosity of a play (in both the French
and the Italian edition it runs to more than 250 pages!) bears little resemblance to
Paolo Baglione, and goes far beyond the aesthetics of realism and symbolism,
which influenced Marinetti's early poetic œuvre. *Le Roi Bombance* carries the
subtitle, 'a hilarious tragedy'. But it was equally a satire on social and political
questions, a parable with strong philosophical undertones, a travesty of other
theatrical traditions (particularly of *grand guignol*), and a parody of a large number
of literary and dramatic genres: the fairy tale, the morality play, *commedia
dell'arte*, farce, *sotie, conte rabelaisien*, etc.

   With such a mixture of genres and traditions all joined together, it is impossible
to interpret the play on one level alone. *Le Roi Bombance* is hardly a *pièce à thèse*
with a clear message. The plot, characters and apothegms are multi-faceted in their
meaning, and care must be taken before ascribing to the author any of the
viewpoints uttered in the play.

   A possible access to the play can be gained via an interpretation of its original
title, *Les Marmitons sacrés*. *Marmite* (cooking pot, and hence, *marmiton*, kitchen
boy) was a satirical description often employed in the late-nineteenth century[170] for
a left-wing activist, whose policies were geared towards satisfying the fundamental
material demands of the working classes. *Les marmites de l'avenir* were the
Socialists and Marxists, who believed that they had found the recipe for the 'soup
of universal happiness'. In *Le Roi Bombance*, the 'cooks of universal happiness'
were the reformist Socialist, Filippo Turati, the intransigent Socialist, Enrico Ferri,
and the Revolutionary Syndicalist, Arturo Labriola, to whom the Italian edition of
the play was dedicated. However, this dedication should not commit the reader to
an all-too narrow interpretation. As Marinetti said in his letter to Pascoli, quoted
below, the play was based on his 'observations of the socialist movement in
Europe', and not only in Italy. Therefore, the three Cooks could also have
represented Guesde, Jaurès, and Millerand.

   On this level, the play can be read as a political satire about a failed revolution
and the political pretensions that accompany it. As I mentioned above, Marinetti
had closely observed the social unrest of 1898 and the General Strike of 1904, and
the rôles played by the socialist, syndicalist and anarchist leaders in these events.
The weak, incompetent and dim-witted King is an allusion to Vittorio Emanuele II;

---

[170] See the examples given in Lista, *La Scène futuriste*, p. 36.

the royal counsellors bear resemblance to Giolitti; and the chaplain, who knows no loyalty to anything but his own stomach, stands for the Catholic Church as the chief advisor of the Italian monarchy. On this level, Le Roi Bombance offers a satirical comment to the political developments of post-risorgimento Italy. The Socialists offer grandiose promises to the starving masses, but once they have reached the lower echelons of political power (in November 1903, Turati was offered an insignificant position in Giolitti's government), they want to take over the government and run the country. Despite their revolutionary rhetorics, they remain loyal servants to the King and try to appeal both to the monarch and the people. They lead the 'intestinal revolution' only in order to gain positions of power for themselves.[171] The 'revolution' of the marmitons leads to anarchy, savagery and an orgy of violence, which eventually brings about the restoration of the old régime (just as the failed strike of 1904 and the ensuing chaos strengthened Giolitti's government).

Not all that different from the Scullery-Boys is the anarchical leader of the hungry masses, Estomacreux, based on the syndicalist Labriola.[172] He is equally corrupt, and ready to strike a deal with the Socialists when they promise him a cabinet position in their revolutionary government. He is a dim-witted braggart, whose revolutionary zeal is unchannelled and without vision. Like the hungry masses, his actions are determined by the stomach. Even his revolutionary rhetorics cannot hide his base material instincts: 'Let Justice, Equality and Liberty finally reign in all stomachs and in all intestines!' (p. 246) is his ultimate political

---

[171] In a statement published in 'Risposta all'inchiesta "I nostri scrittori in villeggiatura"' in Verde e azzurro, 1, no. 26 (October 1903), Marinetti reports: 'Ho condotto a termine Les Marmitons sacrés, una tragicommedia in quattro atti di un sarcasmo spietato contro lo sfruttamento attuale delle folle bêtes et moutonnières.'

[172] On Labriola see the critical literature listed in note 69. His views on Le Roi Bombance were published in Avanti! of 23 October 1905: 'Molti di noi lo [i. e. Marinetti, G.B.] sanno frequentatore delle assemblèe socialiste, delle radunate pubbliche, delle agitazioni popolari e partecipe anche di certi commovimenti nazionali, che rasentano lo stato rivoluzionario. Forse ci viene come esteta in cerca di emozioni e forse anche come un dubbioso od un scettico non tranquillo in cerca d'una fede, ma certo non l'ha trovata, perché anzi il conoscere quelle fedi novelle e il contatto delle folle esaltate hanno aggravato il suo pessimismo e reso più amaro il sarcasmo col quale si esprime. La conoscenza delle forme ancora in gestazione della vita sociale lo ha persuaso che ciò che a molti appare nuovo e benefico é antiquato e già corrotto e gravido di mali impensati. E così ha chiesto alla ricca fantasia, al sicuro istinto dell'arte i mezzi per comporre il lugubre ditirambo delle novelle illusioni delle quali si pasce una parte tanto larga dell'enorme gregge umano. E l'opera d'arte c'é.' He goes on to offer a résumé of the plot and concludes: 'Su questo macabro torso, F. T. Marinetti ha buttato il manto reale della sua fantasia ricca d'immagini e di parole, una vera fantasia di poeta, che sa trovare un elemento di bellezza pur nell'uso della più ingrata e rivoltante materia. La tesi del Marinetti vale quel che vale. Il pessimismo é un sentimento antico quanto l'uomo e un vecchio motivo di ispirazioni artistiche. La sua migliore confutazione é nel fatto stesso della esistenza e del movimento della Storia. Ma tesi a parte, poche opere in questi ultimi tempi saranno apparse più strane, più originali, più suggestive e preoccupanti della bizzarra tragedia, sul quale ho cercato di richiamare l'attenzione del lettore.' Labriola also reviewed the first production of the play in Avanti! of 10 April 1909.

programme.[173] He is not a leader of a revolution, but only of a popular revolt that leads to anarchy and chaos. This, however, is not altogether negative. As he himself declares: 'Violence is a midwife with blood running down her arms, who from a dying womb pulls forth the future, a radiant baby!' (p. 111) Potentially, Estomacreux and the Hungry Ones can play an important rôle in the overthrow of the old order; but because of their ignorance and lack of discipline they also endanger the successful outcome of the revolution. And because of their base materialism and anti-intellectual attitude, they are eternal enemies of art, poetry, and intellectual achievement.

This interpretation of the play's political and social topicality is supported by a letter Marinetti wrote to Pascoli in May 1905:

> Le Roi Bombance is the result of two years of meditation and observation of the socialist movement in Europe. The work was conceived one hot summer evening in a large popular meeting poisoned with brutal stupidities and alcoholized with the reddest eloquence. During one of these oratorial duels, Turati (who resembles my reformist Béchamel in the play) and Labriola (who resembles, with more talent, my revolutionary Estomacreux) offered a spectacle to 3,000 Milanese workers. The play was finished during the General Strike in Milan. I have demonstrated with the means of the burlesque the tragic and fatal victory of idealist individualism over the brutal masses, employing an inexhaustible pessimism in my description of the invincible imbecility of the people and the ferocity of human nature. In short, I have concluded the play with the bankruptcy of socialism, the glory of anarchism, and the complete derision of the reformist and other promise-mongers parading as cooks of the universal happiness. The tragedy has only one fantastic character: Saint Putrefaction, a terrifying spectre formed by the pestilent fumes emanating from the Ponds of the Past. The spectre appears amongst the vapours of a colossal orgy, where the Hungry Ones, having finally (in the third act) found something to eat, dream in their drunken state of devouring the cadavers of the King and his courtiers. Essentially, Le Roi Bombance is nothing but a tragedy of hunger (in all its forms) and a cruel satire on all intermediaries, demagogues and other go-betweens of the stupid masses, eternally striving for the impossible happiness.[174]

This statement reveals that the play is not at all comparable to the social drama of the nineteenth century (Hauptmann's The Weavers, Zola's Germinal, etc.), nor does it really address the topic of 'les foules modernes', as Lista suggests.[175] The social unrest of the period was only a backdrop, onto which Marinetti projected a

---

[173] There are again clear parallels to Nietzsche's Zarathustra, who also opposed all egalitarianism ('Ye preachers of equality, the tyrant-frenzy of impotence crieth thus in you for 'equality': your most secret tyrant-longings disguise themselves thus in virtue-words!' Book II, ch. 29 — The Tarantulas). Although he regards hedonistic pleasures an integral part of human nature, it is a disgrace to live purely for the stomach ('Life is a well of delight. But to him in whom the upset stomach speaketh, the father of affliction, all fountains are poisoned.' Book III, ch. 56 — Old and New Tables — § 16).

[174] The letter is printed in Giovanni Lista, Marinetti et le futurisme. Etudes, documents, iconographiques (Lausanne, 1977), p. 63. In another letter to Gustavo Botta, published by Carlo Martini in La fiera letteraria of 30 September 1962 he wrote: 'Ho derivato il personaggio di Béchamel da Turati, quello di Syphon da Ferri. Quello di Estomacreux é una sintesi di Labriola-Lazzari-Braccialarghe e molti altri. Del resto capirai perfettamente la quantità d'osservazioni dirette e di libera intuizione che contengono tutti i personaggi del Roi Bombance. Le Roi, per esempio, si trova al primo atto nelle condizioni d'un qualsiasi re italiano all'indomani della morte di un Crispi.'

[175] In La Scène futuriste, p. 35.

political and ideological message he had developed primarily from the sources described in the first part of this essay.

As his portrayal of the three Scullery Boys in *Le Roi Bombance* shows, Marinetti shared many of Sorel's views on institutionalized Party socialism (see above, pp. 25–26). But how does Estomacreux, the syndicalist leader, fit into the picture? Clearly, Marinetti did not have much faith in Italian syndicalism and did not view it as a revolutionary movement in Sorelean terms.[176] His political theory was far more anarchical than that of Labriola. Hence the necessity in the play to find a counterbalance to the socialist characters. This is where the symbolic figure of the Poet and the allegorical characters of Saint Putrefaction and Ptiokaroum come into play. They represent a philosophy of life which Marinetti derived mainly from Nietzsche, whose *Thus Spake Zarathustra* he appears to have read during this period.

FIG. 11.   Marinetti (second from left) receives the Poet's Laurels at a literary convention in the Teatro Regio of Parma, 1906.
Caricature by N. Musini

How intensive Marinetti's studies of Nietzsche's writings were is impossible to ascertain. He seems to have come across them during his student years, for there are clear references to Nietzschean concepts in many of his poems, as I have shown above. The Poet/Idiot figure in *Le Roi Bombance* appears to have been lifted straight out of *Thus Spake Zarathustra*. The *Song of Melancholy* in Book IV describes a very similar 'seeker of truth', who

> from mask of fool confusedly shouting,
> circumambulating on fabricated word-bridges,
> on motley rainbow-arches,
> 'twixt spurious heavens
> and spurious earths,
> round us roving, round us soaring, —
> *Mere* fool! *Mere* poet!
> [...]

[176] Revolutionary Syndicalism in Italy, in marked contrast to its French equivalent, was not principally opposed to political parties (it developed from within the Socialist Party and remained part of the PSI until, in 1907, the followers of Labriola were faced with expulsion), nor against participation in elections (Labriola ran for Parliament in 1904). The leadership was also quite hostile to anarchism and placed formal discipline and structured organization over spontaneous popular insurrection.

In wild forests
Amongst the motley-speckled beasts,
shouldst move, obsessed and wistful,
sinful-sound and comely-colourful,
with longing lips smacking,
blessedly mocking, blessedly hellish, blessedly bloodthirsty,
stealing, sneaking, peeping: -
[...]

Unto eagles like and panthers like
are the poets' desires,
are *your* desires beneath a thousand guises
Thou fool! Thou poet![177]

Nietzsche's poet is a forerunner of the true human being, the *Übermensch*, which Zarathustra describes as follows:

I teach you the Übermensch. Man is something that is to be surpassed. What have you done to surpass him? All beings hitherto have created something higher than themselves; and you are content to be the ebb of that great tide and would rather relapse into the beast than surpass man. [...] Man is a rope stretched between the animal and the Übermensch, — a rope over an abyss.[178]

The *Übermensch* represents human perfection attained by crossing the 'abyss' and 'surpassing' oneself. He has brought his human potential to full realization and has become 'the highest type of free man'.[179] He can only do so by 'overcoming' the forces of conformity and corruption, which impede the development of the 'herd-man' in the present, mediocre form of civilization. He is, therefore, a warrior, a man in revolt: against the priests,[180] against the scholars,[181] against women.[182] He opposes virtuousness,[183] faintheartedness, and mediocrity[184] and all other virtues of 'the great majority, the common-place', the 'mumblers and mollycoddles', who live in 'a city of shopkeepers, where floweth all blood putridly and tepidly and frothily through all veins. So spit on their city, which is a great slum where all the scum frotheth together! Spit on the city of pusillanimous souls and frail bodies!'[185]

---

[177] My translations follow, but do not necessarily adhere to, Oskar Levy's edition of *The Complete Works of Friedrich Nietzsche*. I have quoted my references in a manner which enables the reader to locate the passages in any of the many German or English editions available.
[178] *Zarathustra*, Prologue, § 3 and 4.
[179] *Twighlight of the Idols*, Book 9, § 38.
[180] 'Bad enemies they are. Nothing is more revengeful than their meekness. [...] False values and fatuous words: these are the worst monsters for mortals. [...] Verily, rather would I see a shameless one than the distorted eyes of their shame and devotion.' *Zarathustra*, Book II, ch. 26 (The Priests).
[181] 'Their virtues are even more repugnant to my taste than their falsehood'. *Zarathustra*, Book II, ch. 38 (The Scholars). 'Be on the guard against the Learned. They hate you because they are barren.' *Zarathustra*, Book IV, ch. 73 (The Higher Man), § 9.
[182] 'I hate thee most, because of your attraction. [...] Thou art a most dangerous plaything. [...] So if thou goest to women, do not forget thy whip.' *Zarathustra*, Book I, ch. 18 (Old and Young Women).
[183] 'Virtue makes modest and tame'. *Zarathustra*, Book III, ch. 49 (The Reducing Virtues), § 2.
[184] 'Modestly embracing a small happiness — that is submission [...] that is cowardice [...] that is mediocrity'. *Zarathustra*, Book III, ch. 49, § 2.
[185] *Zarathustra*, Book III, ch. 52 (The Apostates) and 51 (On Passing By).

Zarathustra preaches to his followers the doctrine of destruction and creation, of abolishing the Old and building the New:

> And I bade them overturn the old academies where self-conceit and arrogance reigned. I bade them laugh at the great moralists and poets, the great saints and saviours, at the gloomy sages and whoever sat as an admonishing scarecrow on the tree of life. I sat amongst their great ruins, beside the carrion and vultures, and I laughed at their past and its mellow decaying glory. [...] Then flew I quivering like an arrow with sun-intoxicated rapture, out into distant futures [...]. I taught them to create the future and to redeem through their creation everything that has been. [...] Oh my brethren, I consecrate you and teach you to become a new élite. Ye shall be procreators and cultivators and sowers of the future.[186]

They will form the race of the future, where the madness and rationality of millenniums is brought to a union, and they will destroy the rule of 'nonsense and lack of sense':

> Let the value of everything be determined anew by you. Therefore, ye shall be fighters, ye shall be creators. [...] There are a thousand paths that have never been trodden; there are salubrities and hidden islands of life that need be discovered. Man and man's world is still unexhausted and waiting to be explored. Awaken and hearken, ye lonesome ones! From the future comes wind with stealthy pinions, and to sensitive ears good tidings are proclaimed. Ye lonesome ones of today, ye who have been excluded: ye shall one day be a people, the elected from the elected, and from you a chosen people shall arise, and out of it the Superman.[187]

Nietzsche's *Übermensch* is a person who knows that idealist transcendality is a chimera. Therefore, he gives himself wholeheartedly to the tangible pleasures of life.[188] For him, life is love, and love is madness.[189] He, himself, is 'the bolt of lightning that is madness'.[190] And this madness will bring about total liberation:

> This freedom and celestial serenity did I put like an azure bell above all things, when I taught that 'above them and through them willeth an eternal will'. This wantonness and folly did I put in place of that will when I taught that 'in everything there is one thing impossible: rationality'. A *little* bit of rationality, however, a germ of wisdom scattered from star to star, this leaven is mixed in all things: for the sake of folly, wisdom is mixed in all things. [...] This is now heaven's purity unto me, that there is no eternal reason spider and reason cobweb.[191]

However, in order to achieve this 'heaven's purity' the present state of existence has to be overturned:

---

[186] *Zarathustra*, Book III, ch. 56 (Old and New Tables), § 2, 3, 12.

[187] *Zarathustra*, Book I (The Bestowing Virtues), § 2.

[188] 'I beseech you, my brethren, remain true to the earth, and believe not those who speak unto you of other-wordly hopes! Poisoners they are, [...] despisers of life, decaying and poisoned, of whom the earth is weary: So away with them!' *Zarathustra*, Prologue, ch. 3. See also Book I, ch. 3 (The Despisers of the Body).

[189] 'It is true, we love life, not because we are wont to life, but because we are wont to love. There is always some madness in love. But there is also always rationality in madness.' *Zarathustra*, Book I, ch. 7 (Reading and Writing).

[190] *Zarathustra*, Prologue, ch. 3.

[191] *Zarathustra*, Book III, ch. 48 (Before Sunrise).

My brethren, will ye suffocate in the fumes of their maws and cravings? Better go and break their windows and jump into freedom! Avoid their bad odour; flee the fumes of their human sacrifices. [...] For great souls there beckons a free life. [...] There, where the State ceaseth — there only commenceth the man who is not superfluous. [...] There, where the State *ceaseth* — pray look thither, my brethren! Do ye not see it, the rainbow and the bridges of the Superman?[192]

In a truly anarchist fashion he proclaims:

A State? What is that? Well, open your ears and listen, for I will say unto you my word concerning the death of people. A State is called the coldest of all cold monsters. It proclaims cold lies, and these lies creep from its mouth: 'I, the State, am the people!' It is a lie! [...] The State lieth in all tongues of good and evil. Whatever it saith it lieth; and whatever it hath it hath stolen. False is everything in it. With stolen teeth it, the biting one, biteth. False are even its bowels. [...] The State I call it, where all, the good and the bad, are poison-drinkers; where all, the good and the bad, lose themselves; where the slow suicide of all — is called 'Life'.[193]

Therefore, the 'new race' who are 'weaving the cloth of all human future'[194] are no 'reformists', who seek to gain power in the political and cultural establishment:

Just look at these superfluous ones! They steal the works of the inventors and the treasures of the the wise. Culture, they call their theft — and everything becometh sickness and trouble unto them. Just look at these superfluous ones! Sick are they always; they vomit their bile and call it a newspaper; they devour one another, and cannot even digest themselves. [...] Power they seek for, and above all, the levers of power, much money — these impotent ones! See how they clamber, these nimble apes! They clamber over one another, and thus scuffle into the mud and the abyss. Towards the throne they all thrive: it is their madness — as if happiness sat on the throne! Oftentimes filth sits on the throne, and the throne sits on filth. Madmen they all seem to me, and clambering apes, and all-too eager.[195]

Rather, they wage war on the State and on all those who try to uphold the present system. They are like a 'storm that comes and shakes all this rottenness and corrosion from the tree.'[196] This war is seen as a 'necessary evil'[197] and 'a justification of life itself'.[198] Zarathustra's advice is:

Your enemy shall ye seek; your war shall ye wage: for the sake of your thoughts! [...] I advise not to work, but to fight. I advise not to peace, but to victory. Let your work be a fight, and your peace be a victory. [...] Ye say it is the good cause which halloweth even war? I say unto you: it is the good war which alloweth every cause.[199]

Nietzsche's philosophy found an attentive student in Marinetti, and Zarathustra's advice did not go unheeded by the Poet in the play. That is not to say that he was already the *Übermensch* Nietzsche presented as a model. The poet is listed

[192] *Zarathustra*, Book I, ch. 11 (The New Idol).
[193] Ibid.
[194] Zarathustra, Book III, ch. 49 (The Belittling Virtues), § 3.
[195] *Zarathustra*, Book I, ch. 11 (The New Idol).
[196] *Zarathustra*, Book I, ch. 21 (Voluntary Death).
[197] *Zarathustra*, Book I, ch. 5 (Joys and Passions).
[198] *Zarathustra*, Book I, ch. 6 (The Pale Criminal).
[199] *Zarathustra*, Book I, ch. 10 (War and Warriors).

amongst the dramatis personae as *L'Idiot*. This is not, as one might initially assume, an altogether negative characterization. In *Dans les cafés de nuit*, Marinetti informs his Soul that 'geniuses and idiots hold their hands and dance together in a circle' (p. 230). They are two faces of the same coin and reflect Zarathustra's advice of mixing wisdom and madness in the right proportions. But the Poet is not the Superman. Because of his idiocy, the poet is ignorant of any everyday reality and secondly falls into the trap of aspiring to the wrong goals. The beauty of his art does not have the power of enchanting the masses. They are like 'animals' (p. 73) and do not understand his 'ideas dressed in images and symbols' and the 'beautiful clothes of light cut with elegant precision' (p. 72). The power of his 'astral fire' is helpless against the people's 'impure stomachs' (p. 74). Although he has been 'blessed by the Stars, my custodians and guides' (p. 82) and although he belongs to 'the few, the ones elected from the elected, the Saints' (p. 75), his 'sonorous and enraptured song' (p. 75) is fighting a hopeless battle against the din of the ignorant masses. He is tortured and ridiculed by the people and has to go and talk to the birds instead. The poet is full of romantic sentimentalism; he is melancholic and unhappy about the fact that nobody understands him. So he fixes his eyes on the azure horizon, gazes at the stars and the moon, and gets totally lost in the pursuit of his unattainable ideals.

This is a central flaw, which, as we have seen, Marinetti criticized repeatedly in his early poetry. In *La Conquête des étoiles* the main fault of the star-gazers is that they lose sight of the pleasures of the body. Here, in *Le Roi Bombance,* the material pursuits of the masses are characterized as equally negative, but only because they are reduced to the demands of the stomach. What is required is an equilibrium between both spheres of the mind and the body, as the Soul learns towards the end of *Dans les cafés de nuit*. The poet does have the potential of reorienting his hitherto ill-guided desires towards more realistic goals. However, individualistic fulfilment is not granted to him in the end. But he proves that he has learned the lesson from Zarathustra and becomes a messiah of the *Übermensch*. After his resurrection in the fourth act he offers an example of how 'absolute freedom', the quest for the 'Infinite, where time and space lose their name' (p. 251), can be attained. His suicide is a messianic gospel for future generations: with the lyre in his left hand and the sword in his right, he personifies a union of Art and Revolution. His free choice to die is the ultimate affirmation of liberty. For this reason he is the only person who at the end of the play does not join the eternal chain of recurrence.

If the poet exemplifies Marinetti's existentialist vision of the Individual, the allegorical figure of Saint Putrefaction is a representative of the universal law of Nature. Again, the first impression of this character appears to be negative. Her association with the Moon and the Ponds of the Past give her the appearance of a spectre that haunts mankind and draws them into the abyss of primeval morass. Although dramatically she has all the character traits of Evil in the medieval morality play, she also symbolizes a philosophy which Marinetti seems to have embraced at this period. I mentioned above Nietzsche's concept of destruction as a Dionysian, life-giving force. In Saint Putrefaction, Marinetti illustrates another central category of Nietzschean philosophy: *die ewige Wiederkunft* (eternal return[200]).

Nietzsche's *Übermensch* belongs to the Dionysian world that is eternally reborn from the primeval sources of Being. 'Everything goes, everything comes back; eternally rolls the Wheel of Being',[201] says Zarathustra, the 'teacher of eternal recurrence'.[202] He compares life to 'a sand-glass: ever turn it up anew, and anew it runs down and runs out'.[203] There is no passing away that is not re-awakened: ' "Now do I die and disappear", wouldst thou say, "and in a moment I am nothing. The soul is as mortal as the body." But the nexus of causality returns, in which I am intertwined. It will again create me. I myself pertain to the causes of eternal return.'[204] Because of this eternal law of existence we can embrace death with the thought: 'Was *that* life. Well, then! Once more!'[205] Being is not seen as an *Untergang* ('going-down'), but only as a *Übergang* ('going over'). Equally, man as an *Untergehender* is at the same time an *Hinübergehender*. Death is nothing but 'crossing over a bridge'; and Zarathustra loves the man who crosses the bridge 'as a free spirit and with a free heart'.[206] Zarathustra therefore preaches the doctrine of Voluntary Death:

> To treat death as a festival is best; the next best, however, is to die in battle, and sacrifice a great soul. Nothing is more hateful to the fighter and the victor alike than grinning death stealing towards us like a thief, yet coming as a master. Unto you, I praise the voluntary death, which comes to me because *I* want it. [...]. Free for death and free in death. A holy Nay-sayer, when there is no longer time to say Yea: this is a man who has grasped the meaning of life and death.[207]

In *Le Roi Bombance*, Saint Putrefaction relates this 'tragic wisdom' in an extended pontification, which is the exact opposite of the superficial and illusionary interpretation of the world laws by the revolutionaries:

> They [the Hungry-Ones] are my children, the beloved children of Saint Putrefaction [...]. I have breathed into them the bitter fever, the exasperating quest for life, [∴..] the ancient, delusive desire, the old, ardent dream, powdery and smooth, which runs through the fingers like sand[208] [...]. I am incessant life, which bubbles in the inevitable death of exhausted cells. I am the life of the masses, which is reborn in the life of the individual [...].

---

[200] See Oscar Ewald, *Nietzsches Lehre in ihre Grundbegriffen: Die Ewige Wiederkunft des Gleichen und der Sinn des Übermenschen* (Berlin, 1903); Karl Löwitt, 'Nietzsche's Revival of the Doctrine of Eternal Recurrence', in *Meaning in History* (Chicago, 1949), pp. 214–22; D. Bannerjee, 'The Indian Origin of Nietzsche's Theory of the Eternal Return', in *German Life and Letters*, 7 (1954), 161–69; Karl Löwitt, *Nietzsches Philosophie der ewigen Wiederkehr des Gleichen*, 2nd rev. edn (Stuttgart, 1956); Joan Stambaugh, *Nietzsche's Thought of Eternal Return* (Baltimore, 1972); *Nietzsche: A Collection of Critical Essays*, ed. by Robert C. Solomon (Notre Dame, Indiana, 1980), pp. 316–57; Freny Mistry, *Nietzsche and Buddhism: Prolegomenon to a Comparative Study* (Berlin, 1981).
[201] *Zarathustra*, Book III, ch. 57 (The Convalescent), § 2
[202] *Zarathustra*, Book III, ch. 57 (The Convalescent), § 2.
[203] Ibid.
[204] Ibid.
[205] *Zarathustra*, Book IV, ch. 79 (The Drunken Song), § 1.
[206] *Zarathustra*, Prologue, § 4.
[207] *Zarathustra*, Book I, ch. 21 (Voluntary Death).
[208] Nietzsche makes the same comparison with a sand-glass (*die ewige Sanduhr des Daseins*) in *Fröhliche Wissenschaft* § 341.

I am Death embracing Life. I am Death in Life, both joined together like a couple [...]. I am the Goddess of Fecundation and Destruction [...]. I am the absolute and single force, which remains always identical to itself [...]. I am the originator of insurrection [...]. I am the triumphant Goddess of orgies [...]. Where I appear, the rhythm of life accelerates frenetically and Destruction hastens the speed of carnage. This trident symbolizes my triple force: Creation, Destruction, Regeneration. What you call death is nothing but one of many mutations, which in their succession constitute life. (pp. 244–47)

Another central aspect of this philosophy of life is recited in the form of a lesson by Saint Putrefaction's spiritual child, Ptiokaroum. It is the doctrine of 'the eternal road of thirst and hunger':

Desire, desire. Holy fervour of eternal hunger [...] Embracing all beings and things in a vast dream of love, without stopping for possessing any of them. Consume oneself in the ardent desire for the succulent and luminous aspect of the world. Is this desire good or bad? What does it matter? What is essential is the act of desiring [...] Nature has no other Suns but our divine senses. Who cares where our ecstasies come from, as long as they come [...] Our palate and our coveting tongue grow the seed, sweeten the grapes, and prepare the future vintage [...]. The Future? Here we have our sole religion! [...] To enrich oneself with every desire, every hunger, every thirst: this is the delightful torture, the sad happiness, and the whole bitter essence of human existence. Is there any aim to life? The world cannot have one, otherwise she would be limited. (pp. 248–50)

This 'desire' and 'eternal hunger' is, of course, just another term for what Nietzsche called 'Dionysian life force' and Bergson 'élan vital'. They believed in an ontological principle of dynamism and posited a moving power as the primal force (*Urtrieb*) behind the eternal cycle of struggle and strife which we call 'life'. Marinetti shared this philosophy of a dynamic life force as the motor of the universe that gives energy to creation and prevents it from falling into stagnation.

The final image of the play sums up Marinetti's interpretation of this fundamental law of existence: Ptiokaroum drowns the world in blood. Blood is a life-giving substance. And death is a necessary precondition for new life to flourish. Death has an important function in this eternal dynamism of the universe. Like revolution, like the revolt of the Hungry-Ones, *sub specie aeternitatis* it forms part of the 'eternal law of recurrence'. Marinetti was therefore far from judging the anarchical chaos in the play as entirely negative. After all, the play was dedicated to the anarchist poet Paul Adam. He and other anarcho-symbolist artists combined their destructive stance with the constructive pursuit of artistic beauty. Likewise, Marinetti's Poet holds the lyre together with the sword in his hands. He prefigures the Futurist artist, 'elected from the elected ones', the élite of the élite, who will join art and life and carry out a revolution in both spheres.

Marinetti's stance against cultural antiquarianism and socio-political stagnation, which he expressed in his early theoretical writings of 1899–1901 (see above, pp. 41–44) and his first collections of poetry, led him into a delirium of revolt and a desire for the Absolute. The unsatisfactory conditions of the *vie moyenne* had to be overcome in a liberating act of destruction, which for him took on a poetic, even erotic dimension. But he was immensely critical of the artists' flight into a dream world, where they lost touch with the positive aspects of reality.

In his view, to be a true poet means to endure the tension that exists between the two opposing poles of reality and ideality. He lives in a state of ambivalence, just like Nietzsche's Man is suspended between the realms of material existence and spiritual perfection. Overcoming 'infamous reality'[209] and overcoming oneself is achieved through revolution in art and society. For Marinetti, too, destruction is not *Untergang*, but *Übergang*, i. e. an act of crossing the threshold into a brighter future.

Les Dieux s'ent vont and *La Ville charnelle*

After the publication of *D'Annunzio intime*, Marinetti's literary tastes underwent some major changes. Having discarded Hugo and Zola, he then ejected d'Annunzio from his poetic Olympus. Of the Italian poets only two could still find his admiration: Carducci (to whom he dedicated the first issue of *Poesia*) and Pascoli (whose praise he sang in the same issue of *Poesia*). In order to settle his account with his former hero, Marinetti published *Les Dieux s'en vont, d'Annunzio reste* (Paris: S. Sansot, 1908).

This brochure incorporates the text of his earlier *D'Annunzio intime*, but complements it with an essay on the death of Carducci and Verdi (they are the 'Gods Who Have Gone') and a diatribe on d'Annunzio's recent publications. After a sarcastic account of d'Annunzio's life style, Marinetti offers a devastating critique of his former hero's dramatic *œuvre*. He begins his essay with the question: 'Are G. D'Annunzio's tragedies really theatrical works?'[210] The analysis that follows tries to prove that because of their 'never-ending lyrical tirades' (p. 422) and their 'mania for description' (p. 426) they are 'absolutely bookish' (p. 425). Marinetti criticizes 'the inconsistent mixture of dream and reality, the obvious and over-aesthetical psychology' (p. 427), the 'artificial use of the intervention of fate' (p. 427) and the 'drastic and crude stage-effects' (p. 422). He agrees with Gustave Kahn, who judged the plays to be 'mere *shadows* of drama' (p. 426). His own assessment is even more derogatory and already 'Futurist' in tone: 'One goes to see his plays as if visiting a museum' (p. 429). In the last chapter he compares Carducci's writings with d'Annunzio's and comes to the conclusion that the latter offers nothing but 'glittering poems chiselled and polished like gems; imitative and decorative greenery; sick and plaintive ideas buried under the weight of useless opulence' (p. 436).

Could there be a more damning verdict? It is clear that Marinetti, the champion of modern, dynamic literature, was throwing down the gauntlet at d'Annunzio's feet. He saw himself as the rising star of Italian poetry and drama, and D'Annunzio as a competitor, who had to be pushed aside.

To stake another claim to the Italian Parnassus, Marinetti published a third volume of poetry, *La Ville charnelle* (Paris: E. Sansot, 1908). In contrast to his

---

[209] See the epilogue to *Destruction*: 'Invocation à la Mer Vengeresse pour qu'elle nous délivre de l'infâme réality' [*Scritti francesi*, p. 258].

[210] *Scritti francesi*, p. 421.

earlier two volumes, this collection is nearly exclusively made up of poems that had already appeared, between 1898 and 1908, in various magazines (but mainly in his own review, *Poesia*). It contains four very early works (amongst them the poem that won him the literary prize in 1898[211]), about a dozen poems that had been published over the last couple of years, usually dedicated to his literary friends and masters (Gustave Kahn, Paul Adam, Henri de Régnier, Laurent Tailhade, Paul Fort, Emile Verhaeren, etc.), as well as some recent and some unpublished works.

Because of this mixture of poems from different periods, there is no overriding structure or theme to the book. The title, *The Carnal City*, does not fully encapsulate the content of the collection. There is an erotic theme running through it, usually with an Oriental, Egyptian, décor in the background. But there are also poems with a more philosophical tone, offering variations on themes that had been dealt with in the two previous volumes: the oppressiveness of romantic ideals, the fight between the opposing forces of nature (moon-sun, stars-wind, mountains-sea, etc.), an exultation of the liberating force of death (the whole collection is dedicated 'To my Gravediggers'[212]), the conquest of space and time and infinity. Set against these more traditional poems are a number of items with a distinctly modern setting and dealing with topics that appertain to urban life, industry, technology, speed, dynamism, automobiles, etc. Jannini has aptly characterized the collection as 'a collision between a sensibility "born in Egypt" and the reality of the industrial world which Marinetti encountered in "great Milan"'.[213] In fact, the polarity of eroticism and modernity was neatly summed up in the title of the first Italian edition of 1921: *Lussuria-Velocità* (Lust-Speed).

The first section of the book is made up of new works, which serve as an introduction to the heterogeneous mixture of poems that follow in parts two and three. It offers a setting for the theme of the City of Carnal Pleasures and evokes the lovers' experience of *joie, plaisir, luxure, extase, ivresse* etc. The atmosphere of Oriental decadence is combined with an imagery that lays stress on the wild forces of nature. Love is no sweet and gentle emotion, but an expression of titanic desires. The author describes the 'large and brutal gestures' (p. 282) born out of an 'heroism of blood' (p. 282). The union of the wind and the sea resembles the primitivism in Marinetti's African novel *Mafarka the Futurist* (1909): 'It's so sweet to hurt you, biting into you like into a beautiful fruit in order to eat you with my full mouth, to

---

[211] *Les vieux marins*, originally published in *Anthologie-Revue*, 1, no. 12 (December 1898), now slightly altered and given a new title: *Les Barques mourantes*. In *Scritti francesi*, pp. 326–29.

[212] 'Je dédie ce livre d'amour A MES FOSSOYEURS' (*Scritti francesi*, p. 271). This dedication indicates that Marinetti's belief in the anarchical *beau geste* was still virulent, as he also shows clearly in the verses on p. 351:

> Liberty, oh condor, your immense and dark wingspan
> has the elastic width of the horizon
> I know your flight is equal to my soul
> which is impassioned by its flight towards a Blue
> that is vaster and purer and more overpowering still.
> Kill me, Liberty, I will sing a song in honour of my death.

[213] *Scritti francesi*, p. 27. The terms set in single quotation marks refer to Marinetti's two autobiographies, *A Sensibility Born in Egypt* and *Great Milan, the Traditional and Futurist City*.

drink your tears and the wild bursts of your liquid voluptuousness.' (p. 283) There is no time for romantic chit-chat: 'I want to absorb in one go the rose-coloured vulva embalmed by the astral breath.' (p. 281) Chaste and romantic pining during the nights of full moon are a bane to mankind: the 'long lunar scissors' are lethal darts flung by the 'skeleton of Death' (p. 291), and 'these immobile stars are the implacable nails which hold the weak souls suspended from the cross' (p. 291). As in the previous cycles, the sea is described as the *grande Mer sorcière* and *démoniaque* (p. 291), with whom life is a 'passionate adventure' (p. 292). She is a force of vitality that spurs on the fearless to conquer the future.

The second section of the book consists of eleven *petits drames de lumières*. Some of them have a semi-dramatic quality, not dissimilar to *Nocturne* in the collection, *Destruction*. Because of their brevity, Donald Marinelli has seen in them a move towards a Futurist theatricality:

> Marinetti wanted plays to achieve the dynamic effect a poem creates in just a few stanzas, just as he wanted poetry to have the immediacy of theatre. Futurist theatre had to strive for the synthesis inherent in poetry [...]. Since a poem is supposed to be the innermost, lyrical expression of a poet's thinking, it is freest from the 'demands of technique' that Marinetti claims hampers the theatre playwright whose artform currently 'distorts and diminishes an author's talent'.[214]

The first of the 'Light Plays' resembles 'the short, acted-out poem, the dramatized sensation' Marinetti called for in his *Synthetic Theatre Manifesto*.[215] It has five 'characters', three 'speaking parts', and a chorus. The Vines and Cypresses are entranced by the 'immobile moon' and the 'singing stars'. The Sun chides them for their romantic longings and calls them 'imbeciles'. She explains that the power of the moon will soon wane and eventually be destroyed by the rays of dawn. The second playlet enlarges upon the theme of this cosmic drama, the fight between moon and sun. The third is called 'The Director Amuses Himself' and has as its protagonist 'the director of the review *Poesia*' (p. 311), who engages in an argument with the moon. The fourth is an allegory of the 'small, young boats', who leave behind the 'old fortresses in the port' and begin an adventurous journey on the sea. Here, they experience 'hideous sorrows (so what?)', but also the pleasure of having 'savoured everything and cursed the lot (so what the hell?)' (p. 317). Drawn by the voice of Aurora, they throw themselves 'towards the isles of absurdity and the infinity of the seas' (p. 319). The 'wind of liberties' swells their sails. The atmosphere is 'filled with horror and with elastic hopes' (p. 320) as they fulfil their 'dreams of smiling and vermilion folly, [...] of brutal lust and carnage, [...] of absurd suicide and adventure' (p. 320).[216] As Jannini aptly comments: 'For

---

[214] Marinelli, *Origins of Futurist Theatricality*, p. 299.
[215] TeI 104 (Flint 128).
[216] There is again a striking similarity in *Thus Spake Zarathustra*, where the men of the future are forced to leave the fortress of false security and embark on a dangerous and frightening sea journey in order to discover 'our children's land', the 'country of man's future'. See book III, ch. 56 — Old and New Tables — § 28.

Marinetti, this adventure will be called Futurism.'[217] The image of immobile fortresses is connected with the subheading 'The Uselessness of Wisdom' and the journey of the small boats with 'Victory of Aurora'. What life after the 'New Dawn' will be like becomes apparent in the third section of the volume, called 'Dithyrambs'.

Of these thirteen hymns, the first is of particular interest, because if offers — as Donald Marinelli called it — 'a roadmap leading towards Futurism'.[218] The poem is entitled *A mon Pégase* and was first printed in *Poesia* under the heading *A l'Automobile*. It begins with the lines:

> Vehement god from a race of steel,
> Automobile drunk with space,
> trampling with anguish,
> biting with strident teeth!
> O fearsome Japanese monster with furnace eyes,
> nourished by fire and mineral oils,
> hungry for horizons and astral prey.
> To a diabolical vroom-vroom I unleash your heart
> and your giant wheels, to start the dance
> you perform on the white roads of the world.
> When finally I loosen your metal reins
> you soar, drunkenly,
> into freedom-giving Infinity!

Marinetti goes on to enthuse about speed and acceleration, which excite the driver's feverish desires. He feels totally at the mercy of this 'lovely demon' and wants to be 'joyfully consumed by Infinity'. The mountains try to hold him back, but he overcomes them. The 'gallop of this crazed monster' continues as they cross rivers and plains. Then, the driver lays a wager with the stars. 'Faster, faster still', he spurs on the machine, and 'the pulse of the engine multiplies a hundredfold its élan'. They leave contact with the earth and fly through 'the great bed of heaven'.

In a highly synthesized version, this poem gives a similar impression to that of the 'mad journey' on the 'fantastic tramway' in *Destruction*. By now, however, Marinetti has shed the luxurious and incidental imagery that was characteristic of his previous work in order to concentrate on the intoxicating experience of overcoming the laws of time and space. The main themes of the earlier cycle are still present, but they emerge without encumbering ornamentation or are only alluded to rather than fully elaborated. The demon of speed feels similarly attracted by the Infinite, he has to overcome the same sluggishness of his surroundings, and finally he enjoys the same freedom of flying unencumbered through space. But the idea is expressed on two rather than forty pages.

[217] *Scritti francesi*, p. 30. He sees in this poem a turning point in Marinetti's early career: 'The apocalyptic nightmare gives birth to a bursting desire for life and action, where the dreams are turned into tangible reality. It is a vitalism that is reaching into the future. Because of its strongly activating quality, it is clearly different from d'Annunzio's purely aesthetic superhero-ism. In that sense Marinetti may have been right in setting the date for the beginning of Futurism around 1905, the year in which he published *La Mort des forteresses* in *Poesia*.' p. 28
[218] Marinelli, *Origins of Futurist Theatricality*, p. 175.

The switch from train to car can be explained by the technological progress that improved travelling methods in the first decade of the twentieth century. The opening of the trans-Siberian and trans-African railways was widely reported in Europe; in 1902, it was possible to journey, mainly in trains, around the world in forty days. But the interest in locomotives was soon overtaken by that for automobiles. The number of cars on French roads rose from about 3,000 in 1900 to 50,000 in 1909 and 100,000 in 1913. In 1905, the fastest speed ever recorded was 175 kmph. When Marriott set a new record at 200 kph, the event was described in the newspapers as 'the wonder of petrol motors' that 'punches a hole into space' and looks like 'a ball being fired from a cannon'.[219] In 1907, the Peking to Paris car race was won by two Italians, Scipione Borghese and Luigi Barzini, who described their experience in a book called 'Half the World Seen from an Automobile' (Milan: Hoepli, 1908). The triumphant advance of the automobile found reflection in a large number of literary works, which flooded the market in the earlier part of the century, e. g. Eugène Demolder, *L'Espagne en auto: Impressions de voyage*, Paris 1906; Octave Mirbeau, *La 628-E8*, Paris 1907; Henry Kistemaeckers, *M. Dupont, chauffeur: Nouveau roman comique de l'automobilisme*, Paris 1908 (and the sequels *Aéropolis: Roman comique de la vie aérienne*, Paris 1909 and *Lord Will, aviateur, et autres histoires pour finir avec le roman comique de l'automobilisme*, Paris 1911); Paul Arosa, *Mémoires d'une 50 H.P.*, Paris 1909; Tristan Bernhard, *Les Veillées du chauffeur*, Paris 1909; Paul-Adrien Schayé, *Un Tour de manivelle, et l'on part*, Paris 1909.[220]

Marinetti's own 'comic car novel' was an event described in a note of *Corriere della sera* of 15 October 1908:

> This morning, shortly before twelve o'clock, F. T. Marinetti drove in his automobile through Via Domodossola. The owner of the car was himself at the steering wheel. He was accompanied by the mechanic Ettore Angelini, 23. For unknown reasons, but probably in order to avoid a cyclist, the automobile ended up in a ditch.[221]

Marinetti was lucky to survive the accident with only a shock and his mechanic to get away with a few minor fractures. The experience did not lessen Marinetti's love for cars. He hailed the automobile as a symbol of modern life. This new machine, he proclaimed, would lead mankind to the conquest of the stars and give the final blow to the oppressive reign of the moon. For him, it was the man-made equivalent of the powerful Sea, and would open the gate to Infinity and the future. No wonder, Marinetti saw in the car a demi-god, to whom he could dedicate a dithyramb, just as the Ancients had sung their dithyrambs in honour of the god Dionysus. Both

[219] See the quotes and figures in Pär Bergmann, *Modernolatria*, p. 17.

[220] See Emile Magne, 'Le Machinisme dans la littérature contemporaine', *Mercure de France* (16 January 1910), pp. 202–17 and Paul Ginestier, *Le Poète et la machine* (Paris, 1954). In Germany, the 'car craze' was best reflected in the writings of Otto Julius Bierbaum, *Eine empfindsame Reise im Automobil* (Berlin, 1903); *Das höllische Automobil* (Berlin, 1904); *Mit der Kraft: Automobilia* (Berlin, 1906); *Die Yankeedoodlefahrt und andere Reisegeschichten: Neue Beiträge zur Kunst des Reisens* (Munich, 1910).

[221] Quoted in Salaris, *F. T. Marinetti*, p. 69. See also Marinetti's own account of the event in the *Founding and Manifesto of Futurism* of 1909, TeI 9 (Flint 40–41).

FIG. 12.   Marinetti at the steering wheel of his FIAT in 1908

'gods' were friends and benefactors of the human race and provided them with the means to achieve *ivresse*: for the Ancients it was wine, for the Moderns it was speed. For Marinetti, these gifts were elixirs of life that could conduce man to poetic expression of his vitality. The modern equivalent to the Dionysian dithyramb[222] therefore had to be an ode to the automobile.

In the epilogue to *La Ville charnelle*, Marinetti produced another hymn in praise of the car as a means to conquer the realm of the impossible. It is a prose piece called *La Mort tient le volant* (Death Holds the Steering Wheel; in the first publication in *Poesia* it was entitled *Le Circuit de la jungle*, Jungle Circuit[223]). It was written, as the subtitle indicates, in Brescia on the day of a car race, the 'Contest for the Prize of Speed'.

Here, the themes of primitivism and modernism are drawn together in the image of a negro driver, who boards his 'great metallic jaguar' (p. 368) and races against three 'enormous revolvers on four wheels' and two 'steel mares' (p. 369). As they enter the race course, a 'jungle electrified by a thunderstorm' (p. 368), they are warned that they 'will perish under the cudgel of Death' (p. 368). And indeed, in the track's 'violent river of mud brusquely appears Death' (p. 370). The jaguar sees him

---

[222] It is worthwhile remembering that the poems in Book IV of *Thus Spake Zarathustra* were called *Dionysos-Dithyramben*.

[223] It is used again, tellingly, in the 'Futurism' issue of *Poesia* in 1909, in a translation of the author, entitled *La morte prese il volante (Visione futurista d'una corsa d'automobile)*.

first. It snorts and roars and dashes forward to 'swallow the vast lane and bite the wind in its buttocks' (p. 370). The revolver 'leaps behind him like an exploding drum and screens the horizon with his bursts of speed' (p. 370). They conquer space, and like 'galloping bombs they explode [...], vindictive like the red flags of a revolution'. (p. 370) The frenzied shouts of the drivers mix with the enthusiastic roar of the spectators:

> Faster than the wind, faster than a thunderbolt [...]. It is possible to throw your machine onto the cascade of rain and to soar up to the clouds with strong gusts of the motor [...]. Lift yourself from the earth, you who wants! — Rise to the sky, you who desires! — Triumph, you who believes! — You have to believe and to want! — Oh desire, desire, eternal magnet! — And you, my scorching will-power, great carburetter of dreams! [...] Oh you, my explosive and detonating heart! Who prevents you from vanquishing Death? — Who forbids you to achieve the Impossible? — Make yourself immortal by a stroke of will-power! (p. 371)

The answer is: Nothing. Everything is possible to those who dare. So in the end the metallic jaguar conquers space and 'leaps over the funereal torpedo of Death' (p. 371). Primitive will-power, combined with the technical inventions of the Modern Age, creates a new race to whom belongs the FUTURE.

Poupées électriques

Marinetti's last major publication before the inception of Futurism as an organized movement was a play he had written in 1905–07, *Poupées électriques: Drame en trois acts* (Paris: Sansot, 1909).[224] It was dedicated to the American inventor, 'Wilbur Wright,[225] who knew to elevate our migrant hearts beyond woman's captivating lips'.[226] In an interview with *Comoedia*, reprinted as a preface to *Poupées électriques*, Marinetti declared: 'We want to finally combat the tyranny of love which, especially in the Latin countries, shackles and dries up the creative

---

[224] Lista, *La Scène futuriste*, p. 39 quotes a letter from Marinetti to the theatre director Virgilio Talli, undated, but written shortly after December 1905, in which he reports: 'I'm also in the process of preparing a drama, which is of strong theatrical interest, — particularly to you.' In the June 1907 issue of *Teatro illustrato*, Marinetti's friend Umberto Notari states on p. 212 in an article on *Quello che preparano i nostri autori* that 'in the tranquility of Viggiú [...] the author of *Le Roi Bombance* has completed a play called *I fantocci*'. It was performed, prior to its printing, in Turin on 15 January 1909 in an Italian translation by Decio Cinti, and entitled *La donna è mobile*. The second production by the Compagnia Gualtiero Tumiati at the Teatro dal Verme in Milan in January 1914 carried the title *Elettricità*, and the first Italian edition, which contained only the second act of the French version, was entitled *Elettricità sessuale* (Milan, 1920); reprinted in Marinetti, *Teatro*, vol. 2). When performed at the Teatro degli Indipendenti in Rome, on 28 May 1925, the play changed title again and was now presented as *Fantocci elettrici*.
[225] Wright was the creator of the world's first powered and man-carrying airplane. In 1903 he conducted a European tour trying to interest governments in his invention of a practical and controlled 'Flying Machine'.
[226] F. T. Marinetti, *Poupées électriques: Drame en trois actes avec une préface sur le futurisme* (Paris, 1909), p. 37.

forces of men of action. We want to replace in their imagination the ideal silhouette of Don Juan with that of Napoleon, Andrée[227] and Wilbur Wright.'[228]

Within the framework of a *pièce-bien-faite* revolving around the dramatic device of a love triangle, Marinetti inserted his Futurist vision of a modern world and a critique of the forces of tradition and sentimentality. To do so, he employed a form of theatre that contained all the ingredients hankered after by bourgeois audiences, but his aim was to denounce both the genre and the tastes of these spectators.

The protagonists of the play are John Wilson, an American inventor of robots, and his wife Mary, a sensual Egyptian of Levantine extraction. The autobiographical basis of Marinetti's characterization of their relationship is indicated in the second edition of the play, where the engineer is given the name Riccardo Marinetti. Marinetti's short autobiographical sketch in *Scatole d'amore* contains a description of his 'mad passion' for a girl called 'Mary, pupil at a nun's school attached to our college. She was a Levantine with big liquorice eyes, camelia cheeks, sensual and fleshy lips' etc.[229]

John and Mary used to be a perfect couple, a match of two like-minded spirits. But now their happiness has been disturbed by the intrusion of bourgeois morality. John is a man who combines in himself virility, intelligence and technical genius. Mary is a sensual, passionate, 'Oriental' woman, who follows her animalistic instincts. In the first act, the devastating effect conventional ethic has on human life is demonstrated: Juliette, Mary's friend, is an epitome of romantic sentimentalism and is driven to suicide by her unfulfilled love for a naval officer, Paul de Rozières. However, John and Mary do not heed this warning, and a year later we see that they have also been infected by bourgeois sentiments. John has become jealous and a dreamer, and Mary takes objection to his abnormal sexual fantasies and succumbs to the forces of morbid sentimentality.

The couple's bizarre love games are closely related to John's great invention, the *poupées électriques*. There are many of these marionettes stored in the attic, and two of them we see displayed in the second act. They are called Mother Prunelle and Mister Prudent (in the second edition their names are changed to Professor Matrimony and Mrs Family) and are portrayed as caricatures of the pillars of society. For John they are representatives of 'the ghastly reality of duty, money, virtue, old age, monotony, emotional boredom, physical exhaustion, engrained stupidity, social laws, and who knows what else'.[230] In more concrete terms, the marionettes are a recreation of Mary's Aunt Alice and her father, the Magistrate. They had impeded the couple's amorous pursuits during the time of their courtship and forced John into stealing embraces from Mary whenever the parents were not observing them. Now, many years later, the marionettes are used to evoke and rekindle the former times of young love and illicit passion. Drawing on his

---

[227] Salomon August Andrée was a Swedish explorer who, in 1897, went missing during an expedition to the North Pole carried out in a hot-air balloon.
[228] Ibid., p. 33.
[229] F. T. Marinetti, *Scatole d'amore in conserva* (Rome, 1927), p. 11.
[230] *Poupées électriques*, pp. 134–35.

memories, John's greatest pleasure is to have sex with his wife in the presence of, or rather behind the back of, these representatives of bourgeois respectability. It gives him 'the fever of adventure and of the unknown, the perfume of revolt and danger and the impossible' (p. 135). However, he is more in need of these stimuli for their lovemaking than Mary. Initially, both of them enjoyed the artificial and mechanical recreation of the 'mysteries of love'. The puppets were a congenial invention to keep their rebellious romance alive. (In the second edition, John declares: 'Love is Futurist. It deceives, kills, the slow, the old, the fearful, the stationary. Love is a plot by the young against those who are no longer young. Family and Matrimony: out of the window!'[231]) John has internalized the mechanical aspect of love to such an extent[232] that he can regard Mary as one of his marionettes, 'the most beautiful of all' (p. 132). In the past, both of them shared this taste for an amorous 'electricity that makes our nerves vibrate like conducting wires of lust' (p. 132). Their entire life in the villa 'Monbonheur' was based on this 'prodigious stimulant of the heart' (p. 132). But now things have changed. Mary no longer approves of the 'sentimental application' (p. 131) of John's engineering genius. She explaines to him that she does not need the puppets to get excited and that she wants to be appreciated for her own beauty. Therefore, she implores John to throw the marionettes out of the house.

But before he gets rid of 'these two monsters [...] who have now become useless' (p. 137), John reflects on his need to surround himself with images of ugliness in order to enjoy his escapes into a land of pure fantasy. He cannot sustain his dreams without a palpable reminder of the emptiness of bourgeois existence. It is the 'presence of the odious puppets that gives fascination and beauty to the sea, the clouds, the ships, the birds and the shooting stars on the horizon' (p. 136). The very moment John complies with Mary's wish, his mental attitude changes. What, in the second edition of the play, is interpreted as a Futurist act of rebellion against false sentimentality, appears in the original French version as an act of succumbing to Mary's morality. John gets infected by the same virus, and the consequences of this are displayed in the third act (which is missing in the Italian edition). Here, Paul de Rozières returns and confesses his love for Mary. John gets extremely jealous and behaves like a bourgeois husband, insisting on his marital rights and forcing Mary to obey his orders. But she refuses to submit to his demands. She realizes that love between them is no longer possible. What cannot be attained in the real world any longer she must seek in the heavenly realm. She takes the revolver out of John's hand and shoots herself — following Juliette's example, who had killed herself in the first act in order to follow Paul into the land beyond the horizon.

In a way, the play predates the Surrealists' celebration of de Sade and his uninhibited actualization of the darker, uncivilized side of the libido. Marinetti seems to take a positive view of John Wilson's uncontrolled, unconventional, even bizarre passions. For after all, the puppets are his own creation and testify to his

---

[231] *Elettricità sessuale*, in: Marinetti, *Teatro*, 2, p. 447.
[232] On p. 135 he says about the marionettes that 'they are inside us.'

Futuristic genius. When at the end of the second act he has thrown them out of the window in order to comply with his wife's wish, he is shown to surrender to Mary's newly acquired bourgeois attitudes and to reject his scorn of the representatives of bourgeois respectability. The marionettes are not doubles of his personality, as Lista suggests.[233] When John says in Act II that the marionettes are 'inside us', he is not referring to them as alter egos. The puppets are parental figures who disparage free and uninhibited love and who remind John 'that stolen apples are tastier than bought ones'.[234] They incite his desire for adventure and danger and provide him with 'the perfume of revolt'. The puppets are beautiful because of the perfection of their mechanism. This is why John in Act III, in a bout of sexual desire for his wife, can say that she resembles one of his puppets. But there is an ironic touch to this statement, for Mary, in her moralistic behaviour, has in actual fact become like the figures of bourgeois respectabilty. But maybe, he was dreaming of the 'perfect puppet', an automaton that mechanizes all desires and fulfils to perfection the 'mechanics of love'? It seems that there is no clear-cut meaning behind the puppets' symbolism. But the end of the play ties in with most of Marinetti's early poems. Romanticism is portrayed as a mortal danger. Just as bourgeois mentality destroys the pleasures of life, so excessive sentimentality leads to the abandonment of real love.

Marinetti offered no clues for an obvious meaning of the puppets. Only after five years, on the occasion of the second production of the play, did he intimate a possible interpretation in *Il resto del Carlino* (20 January 1914). Here, he describes Riccardo Marinetti as 'an innovative and destructive brain who finds himself in opposition to society, which judges him to be mad. [...] He is not a boring, ponderous scientist, but a man who loves women, although he carries into his affairs an element that is too logical and refined. He forgets that women are instinctive beings and have to be treated with care. Riccardo is an intellectual, Maria a sensual woman. What gives rise to the drama is the fact that he has introduced these marionettes into their erotic and sentimental life.'[235] The puppets have been invented by him in order to give the couple's love 'a taste of danger and violence.' In their amorous games behind the back of the marionettes, 'Maria feels herself becoming a child again. She loses her voice of an adult woman and reverts to her childish voice.' For Riccardo, the puppets represent 'everything that is stupid, hard and monotonous in life. They stimulate and accentuate, by their contrast, his love [for Maria] and give it an atmosphere of danger and romantic adventure.' But Maria feels that this game has become an imposition on her life and 'instinctively, desires an impulsive love without complications'.

However, in the first, French, version of the play, Mary can hardly be considered a positive character. Only by cutting the third act in the Italian edition and giving

[233] Lista, *La Scène futuriste*, p. 41 draws a parallel with E. A. Poe's short story, *William Wilson* and Saint-Pol-Roux's *Les Personnages de l'individu*. However, I think that their function is quite different from the puppets in Marinetti's *Bianca e Rosa* or the marionettes in Prampolini's *L'ora del fantoccio*.
[234] *Poupées électriques*, p. 112.
[235] The essay is reprinted in Marinetti, *Teatro*, 2, pp. 482–84.

Maria the task of liberating Riccardo from his 'over-logical and refined' fixations, can she appear as a Futurist woman, an *Eve future*, for whom the Marchesa Casati and Valentine de Saint-Point may have offered a model.[236]

The proto-Futurist performances of 1909

Marinetti's career as a declaimer has been dealt with in the previous chapter. Besides giving many poetry readings he also practised his skills as a political orator and engaged himself in the Irredentist movement. In May 1908, a political demonstration took place honouring Guglielmo Oberdan, who in 1882 had attempted to murder the Austrian Emperor and had consequently been executed by the Austrians. He had become a hero of the nationalist and irredentist movements in Italy, and in 1908, when his mother died, the occasion was seized upon to demonstrate for the restitution of Trieste to Italy. Marinetti went to lay a wreath at the tomb of Oberdan's mother and spoke at the Gymnastic Society, defending the Triestine students shot in Vienna and declaring that one day Trieste would have its own university, even against the will of the Austrian government. The whole episode ended in tumultuous fights, and Marinetti was arrested.[237] Besides the political speech, Marinetti also gave several poetry readings, which to some members of the audience appeared to be in marked contrast to his fervent patriotic attitude. When he was interviewed by the Triestine papers *Il piccolo* and *L'indipendente*, he apologized for writing his verses in French and declared that this was only so because French poetry could serve as a beacon towards which Italian art should aspire and which, eventually, it would surpass. He saw it as his duty to direct Italian poets towards the right path and to show them how to achieve poetic domination.[238]

Finally, Marinetti's career as a dramatist, following the aborted attempt to complete a juvenile drama (*Paolo Baglione*) and the publication of two full-length plays, reached a first height with the productions of *Poupées électriques* in Turin and *Le Roi Bombance* in Paris. Both events framed and complemented the publication of the *Founding and Manifesto of Futurism* and offered a first taste of how the ideas, expressed in the manifesto, could be translated into the tangible

---

[236] Both are believed to have been lovers of Marinetti. On the Marchesa see Caroline Tisdall & Angelo Bozzolla, *Futurism*, 2nd edn (London, 1985), pp. 155–56, and Marinetti's novel, *L'alcova d'acciaio* (Milan, 1921), ch. XI. Valentine de Saint-Point had just published, in January 1913, her *Futurist Manifesto of Lust*, following her *Manifesto of the Futurist Woman*, of 1912. On her affair with Marinetti see Gino Agnese, *Marinetti: Una vita esplosiva* (Milan, 1990), pp. 142–43.

[237] See F. Balilla Pratella, 'Il futurismo e la guerra. Cronistoria sintetica', *Vela latina*, 3, no. 46 (18–24 November 1915), p. 1; reprinted in TeI 482–89.

[238] See Vaccari, *Vita e tumulti*, p. 174. It is interesting to note that a year later, on the occasion of the première of *Le Roi Bombance*, Marinetti replied to his critics: 'I have been treated as an Italian. Yes, that's understood, I am Italian, but I did all my studies in Paris and I completed them at the Sorbonne. I have some very French diplomas which permit me to consider myself belonging to a nation which I love. I have always thought, written, and dreamed in French, and I am proud of having supported and spread the glory of French literature through my lectures and the international review *Poesia*.' 'Les funérailles du Roi Bombance', in *L'Intransigeant* (12 April 1909).

FIG. 13.   G. Grandi, Portrait of Marinetti, 1908

reality of 'the new formula of art as action'.[239] In these two productions we can see how Marinetti's notion of theatre and performance art were becoming inextricably entwined with the ideas of Futurism. And indeed, from the inception of the movement onwards, theatre continued to be employed as a privileged medium of expression.

[239] In 'Prime battaglie futuriste' in *Guerra sola igiene del mondo* Marinetti says that on 11 October 1908 he recognized for the first time the need 'to give assault to the theatres and to introduce the fist into the artistic battle. [...] This new formula of *arte-azione* was a law of mental hygiene.' (TeI 201).

The performance of *Poupées électriques* in Turin on 15 January 1909 went down in the chronicles of Italian theatre history as an event comparable to the *bataille de Hernani* and the scandal that surrounded *Ubu Roi*. Marinetti's later claims[240] to have read the *Founding Manifesto* during the performance indicates that he regarded the production as a practical demonstration of the ideas the Futurist movement sought to promote. Of course, he had to decide which of his two plays he was to present first to the Italian public; he was wise enough to assume that *Le Roi Bombance* went far beyond what the Italian audiences could possibly stomach. Their staple diet was bourgeois comedy, i.e. that form of 'digestive' theatre Marinetti hated most and had always opposed. But he had to choose his tactics carefully. All the evidence we possess of the Turin production indicates that there was nothing that could have warned the spectators, or given them reason to suspect, that they were about to witness some extraordinary performance. The modernist French title had been changed to *La donna é mobile*, promising something amusing just like the popular aria from *Rigoletto*.[241] The production company, Andrea Maggi's 'Compagnia Eroica', consisted of routiniers of the boulevard genre,[242] who had other comedies of Sardou, Rostand, Benelli etc. in their repertoire. None of the reviews of *La donna é mobile* indicates that the stage design of the Turin production was in any way different to what one would expect of a popular comedy presented by a commercial touring company.

The only difference was that the author was not an established dramatist. Italian high society was wont to use the opportunity of a première to demonstrate its cultural pretensions and interests in new artistic trends. The first play of one of Italy's most promising poets[243] would always offer material for subsequent dinner-party conversation. So when the unsuspecting audience arrived at the Teatro Alfieri, hoping for an evening of light, yet interesting, entertainment, Marinetti detonated the bomb that was to signal the end of Italian theatre as he knew it. Provocation and scandal were his weapons in the battle he was to wage on the cultural establishment. They were tools with which to stir spectators out of their complacency. *Poupées électriques*, although outwardly disguised in the trappings of 'digestive theatre', gave a first taste of Marinetti's vision of theatre that could play an active rôle in society. The performance of *Poupées électriques* in Turin was a first demonstration of the Futurist concept of theatre as *art-action*, of an art that invaded society and stimulated active responses from the spectators rather than serving as an object of consumption.

---

[240] In *Marinetti e il futurismo*, TeI 507.

[241] 'Un bel titolo, molto promettente' Achille Tedeschi called the work in his review for *L'illustrazione Italiana* (Milan, 24 January 1909).

[242] Amongst them we find three actors who later organized, and performed in, the first professional theatre companies that toured with Futurist plays throughout Italy: Luigi Zoncada, Gualtiero Tumiati, and Annibale Ninchi.

[243] Carlo Camerano in *La scena di prosa* (Milan, 22 January 1909), introduces Marinetti in his review as 'a writer of geniality and experience, although in the theatre he is offering his first passage at arms', and E. A. Berta in *La gazzetta del popolo* (Turin, 16 January 1909), says that he went to the theatre with the expectation of hearing a new dramatic piece applauded and of returning home with material that would be interesting to report on.

The reviews of the memorable performance at the Teatro Alfieri indicate[244] that the first act was received as was to be expected of a play of this kind: some amusement, some criticism, some boredom. Because the acting was not of the highest standard, the audience was not too impressed by the piece (the critic of *La gazzetta del popolo* described the 'majority of spectators' as being 'dissatisfied'). When, after the first act, the author showed himself with the actors in front of the curtain, they were greeted with some applause and a few catcalls. Then, during the second act, the audience became more agitated. Some found the dialogue in the play 'heavy and monotonous'[245] and the actress, who played Mary, was 'ill-treated, interrupted, derided, torn to pieces by ironic signs of approval and serious and ruthless disapprobation'.[246] After the second act, Marinetti took the curtain call on his own and had to face a massive concert of boos and catcalls. Not in the least disenchanted by this response, the author approached the audience and returned their 'compliments' by declaring: 'I thank the organizers of this whistling and hissing concert which profoundly honours me.'[247] Such a provocative gesture at a première in one of Italy's leading theatres was unheard of and was reported, as Marinetti later claimed,[248] in 418 newspaper articles. It certainly brought the house down, as all reviewers testified:

> Marinetti appeared at the proscenium arch, and with a few ironic words thanked his audience for the whistling, saying that he felt most honoured by this. And the audience went into a rage! Somebody shouted: 'Let's go on honouring the audience![249]
> Imagine the uproar that followed these words! There was a long, insistent and interminable hullaballoo unleashed by the most diverse voices, shouts, screams and exaggerated hissing.[250]
> For many years one has not experienced a scene like this in the theatre.[251]

But in the third act things became even worse:

> The audience, at that moment, decided to take revenge and no longer conceded the floor to the actors in this comedy. The curtain had hardly risen, and a rather clamorous obstructionism began which soon turned into burlesque. During the whole act, the audience conducted a hunt on every sentence, every word. They interrupted and commented on the play with continuous sarcasms that made it impossible to understand anything. [...] The actors went through the motions of speaking their text, but their words could not reach the ears of the audience, not even of those who in this uproar had remained calm and serene.[252]

This clamorous reception of the last part of the play came very much to the surprise of the reviewers. The first two acts had been greeted with a 'harsh, but not

---

[244] See Giovanni Antonucci, *Cronache del teatro futurista* (Rome, 1975), pp. 37–41.
[245] *La scena di prosa* (Milan, 22 January 1909), reprinted in Antonucci, *Cronache*, p. 40.
[246] *La stampa* (Turin, 16 January 1909), in Antonucci p. 38.
[247] Marinetti's report on this in *Poesia* of February/March 1909 is confirmed by the review in *La gazzetta del popolo* (Turin, 16 January 1909), Antonucci, p. 37.
[248] Vaccari, *Vita e tumulti*, p.195.
[249] *La scena di prosa* (22 January 1909), in Antonucci, p. 40.
[250] *La gazzetta del popolo*, in Antonucci p. 37.
[251] *Il momento* (Turin, 16 January 1909), reprinted in Antonucci, p. 40.
[252] *La gazzetta del popolo*, loc. cit.

unjust' reaction, which they found quite understandable, given that the play 'contained everything that strains the audience's patience'.[253] The response was noisy, but the theatre displayed an atmosphere of hilarity rather than aggression. There was certainly no indication that a major scandal was afoot. Then, suddenly, the 'battle, the pandemonium, the chaos' broke loose, as *La gazzetta del popolo* wrote in astonishment, and the reviewer of *La scena di prosa* asked equally perplexed: 'One can't quite understand why the audience of the Teatro Alfieri, which normally displays such a correct and patient attitude towards new plays, was so enraged with Marinetti.' The critic of *Il momento* could only marvel: 'We have sat through worse plays in the theatre and supported them with more patience.' So why was there suddenly this uproar? What caused the chain reaction that finally brought the house down on Marinetti?

"Le Roi Bombance„ à l'Œuvre

Dessin de DE LOSQUES
(Extrait du « FIGARO »)

M. Lugné-Poe (*Anguille*)   M. Jehan Adès (*Le Roi Bombance*)

FIG. 14.   *Le roi Bombance* in Paris, Théâtre de l'Œuvre, 1909
Drawing of de Losque reproduced in Poesia

[253] *La stampa*, loc. cit.

It appears that Marinetti had planned the tumult by hiring a claque that was to provoke and add resonance to the audience's reaction. *Il momento* mentions the 'overloud applause of one section of the audience', and Antonucci believes that it was the task of this claque to ensure that the audience was going to be an active partner and not just a passive witness of the proceedings on stage.[254] When, in the second act, the reactions became more and more vociferous, Marinetti decided to confront the audience with his unheard-of address. This 'new gesture in the history of first nights'[255] unleashed the storm in the last act and encapsulated Marinetti's desire to use the stage as a tribune of agitation and an arena for public debate. His provocation turned the mediocre performance of a weak play into a major scandal. It offered a first impression of what Futurist theatre was going to promote with unabating determination over the next twenty years.

Another foretaste of what Marinetti, the Futurist, was to offer his audiences was given at the first production of *Le Roi Bombance*, organized by the Théâtre de l'Œuvre. It was directed by Lugné-Poë and performed from 3–5 April 1909 at the Théâtre Marigny in Paris. The reception of the 'intestinal epic' was such that *Le vrai mondain* could write: 'Our Parisian audience will not forget this spectacle for some time.'[256] The events that surrounded the performances were amply documented in *Poesia* and thereby helped to increase the publicity Marinetti had attracted with the publication of the *Foundation and Manifesto of Futurism*.

It had not been Marinetti's original intention to delay the production for four years after the publication of the text in 1905. Gustave Kahn suggested Lugné-Poë — who in 1896 had had the courage to stage Jarry's *Ubu Roi* at the Théâtre de l'Œuvre — as the only director capable of producing the play.[257] Marinetti prepared his advances to the director by becoming a founding member of the Maison de l'Œuvre. But the extraordinary scale of the play compelled Lugné-Poë to consider a production only if additional funds could be secured. In 1907, when Marinetti inherited the large fortunes of his father, such finances suddenly became available. Marinetti approached the director for a second time, now 'offering to meet the full cost of the production, and desiring that the piece be presented in luxurious décor.'[258] Despite this generous offer, Lugné-Poë was not over-enthusiastic. Only in 1908, when Marinetti set about founding his 'nouvelle école artistique' and sought two theatre companies to give him additional *réclame*, did Lugné-Poë finally agree to stage *Le Roi Bombance* at the Théâtre de l'Œuvre. The production was first announced in the theatre's *Bulletin* of January 1909, with a première date set for the end of March. Since writing the play, Marinetti had altered his ideological outlook and aesthetics and sought to re-interpret the text in a manner that would make a production more relevant to his latest, Futurist, ideas.

[254] See Antonucci, *Cronache*, p. 24, and Livio, *Il teatro in rivolta*, p. 13.
[255] *La stampa*, loc. cit.
[256] All quotation from reviews of the production are taken from the documentation Marinetti compiled for *Poesia*, 5, nos 3–6 (April–July 1909), 38–51.
[257] See *Poesia*, 2, nos 1–2 (February–March 1906), p. 5.
[258] A. F. Lugné-Poë, *Sous les étoiles (1902–1912)* (Paris, 1933), p. 238.

For this reason, he chose to turn the derisory figure of the Idiot (portrayed in the original as a melancholic, star-gazing poet) into a Futurist hero and protagonist of the production, and with some luck and a little persuasion he managed to obtain the prestigious actor, Edouard de Max, for the rôle. However, this celebrity of the French stage dropped the part after a while, probably because he feared that the production would end in a scandal. The replacement, Claude Garry could not carry the same weight as de Max would have lent to the rôle, but at least, with some delay, the play could finally be given its première.[259]

As to the design of the production, every effort was made to underline the parallels to the legendary production of Jarry's *Ubu Roi*. The stage presented exterior and interior scenes simultaneously in one set. The cut-out palm tree of the 1898 production had been turned into a large orange tree, surrounded by furniture that defied any localization or periodization. By mixing various styles, the designer Eugène Ronsin emphasized the allegorical quality of the piece. The costumes were designed by Paul Ranson, who had already been involved with the *Ubu Roi* production. His figurines, which have recently been published by Giovanni Lista,[260] have a certain infantile and medieval quality and reflect very well Lugné-Poë's concept of the play, which he presented in an interview with *Le Figaro*. He found the drama too forceful and advised Marinetti to cool down his temperament and become more disciplined. To give the piece a more light-hearted quality, he asked for a 'picturesque and pleasant décor designed by Ronsin, which no doubt, will help us'. Because Ranson died on 20 February 1909, the final execution of the costumes, as far as one can see from a photograph of the performance, was quite different. The reviews indicated that Eugène Ronsin's stage designs had an extremely harrowing quality. *L'Intransigeant* spoke of 'les plus étranges décors, décor exageré, grossi, rutilant, décors d'horreur bouffonne' (weird, exaggerated, excessive, glaring décor which is at the same time horrific and comical), that were reminiscent of the nightmares Doré drew for Balzac's *Contes drôlatiques*.

As to the acting style employed in the production, the reviews were not particularly informative. Lugné-Poë, in the already quoted interview with *Le Figaro*, mentioned the difficulty for the actors of giving an adequate interpretation of the 'colossal puppets created by the poet. The performers are not used to interpreting such a concept and do not find it easy to adapt to a new formula.' The solution he found resembled the marionette style already employed for *Ubu Roi*: 'The direction is a veritable *tour de force*. Lugné-Poë had managed to make his actors move with comic effect, a bit like puppets or mannequins.' (*L'Intransigeant*) For that reason, during the performance there were shouts of 'C'est du guignol!' (This is marionette theatre!), as *Le Gil Blas* recorded.

The overall impression one receives from the reviews is that the production possessed the qualities of a 'violently satirical farce' (*L'Intransigeant*). *Le Figaro*

---

[259] The première was, as was common in France at that time, officially called the dress rehearsal (*répétition générale*).
[260] The full set in colour can be found in *Lo spettacolo futurista* (Florence s. d. [1989]), pp. 34–37. Black and white reproductions are included in *La Scène futuriste*, p. 44.

compared it to the satirical magazine, *Assiette au beurre*, and *L'Intransigeant* with
political caricatures. Nearly every reviewer drew a parallel with Rabelais, and most
of them with Jarry. But in contrast to these predecessors, the political allusions in
the play were felt to be more topical. *Le Roi Bombance* was considered to be an
attack on the shambolic world of parliamentary democracy on the one hand, and of

(Dessins de A. L. MARTY
Extraits de « COMŒDIA ILLUSTRÉ »)

M. Lugné Poe (*Anguille*)   M. Jehan Adès (*Le Roi Bombance*)   M. Henry Perrin (*Le Père Bedaine*)

M. Claude Garry
(*L'Idiot*)

FIG. 15.   *Le roi Bombance* in Paris, Théâtre de l'Œuvre, 1909.
Drawings of A. L. Marty reproduced in Poesia

socialist politics on the other. *Le Figaro* thought that the play directed the
spectators' attention to the dangers of the 'hydra of anarchism', and *L'Intran-*
sigeant suggested that in the third act 'instead of orgy read: anarchist régime'. *Le*
Provençal de Paris summed up a general opinion when saying: 'The symbolism is
clear: Marinetti wanted to show the futility of revolutions, the failure of parliamen-
tarianism, which leads to the return of tyranny.' *Le Cri de Paris* reported that for
several years Marinetti had taken an interest in the Italian socialist movement and

was presenting in his play 'the complex feelings which trouble our corrupt democracies, imbued with false socialism and bad collectivism'. Parallels were drawn with the followers of the French trade union, C. G. T., a recent strike of postal workers, and with comrade Jaurès and president Fallières. Lugné-Poë himself lent support to these interpretations by stating in his interview that 'the Unions fight for the liberty of the people and risk to burden it with the tyrannic weight of the sword'.

These were, in broad outline, the main features of the production at the Théâtre de l'Œuvre. And how was the play received? Since all reviews mentioned Marinetti as the head of a new artistic movement called Futurism, it is likely that the majority of people who visited the production had read or at least heard of the manifesto published in *Le Figaro* six weeks prior to the opening. Because of this, 'the audience had arrived with the conviction that a "Futurist" — it was Marinetti who founded this School — had to prove something', said *Le Figaro*, and *Le Provençal de Paris* thought that because of this manifesto 'certain critics were negatively predisposed' (*dépourvues de bienveillance*) towards the production. There certainly prevailed an expectation that something other than the norm was going to be presented. The Théâtre de l'Œuvre was known to take risks and to present plays that had been rejected by other theatres. Therefore, expectations ran high, and by the end of the evening everyone was certain that they had witnessed an extraordinary event. *Le Provençal de Paris* judged the 'three nights of battle and fever [...] to have marked [...] a date in the history of riotous theatre evenings'. Many papers drew parallels to the 'Battle of *Hernani*', and most reviewers felt reminded of 'the heroic days of *Ubu Roi*'. *Le Journal des débats* offered a long description of the Jarry première twelve years earlier; other reviewers assumed that the legendary production of *Ubu Roi* was still in everybody's memory and only needed to be alluded to. The audience reactions as described in the papers were certainly very similar:

> The Marigny theatre had more resemblance to a public meeting than a theatrical performance: people yell, shout, imitate animal sounds. During the intermission one spectator stood on his seat and shouted: 'Citizens! The dramatic art is in danger!' (*Gil Blas*)
> Raised arms, cries of rage, sounds of animals. Is this a meeting, a controversial gathering? No, it is the première of *Le Roi Bombance*. (*Le vrai mondain*)
> The spectators shouted at the actors, retorted with unexpected replies and even with rude words. We were back in the heroic times of the Œuvre. (*La Matin*)

L'Action suggests that this uproar was not entirely an improvised affair:

> Certain compatriots of the author led the uproar with a nationalist enthusiasm. As for certain friends of the author, they wanted to give us a second première of *Hernani*.

With the support of this *claque*, Marinetti managed to create an atmosphere of 'general delight' ('joie générale', said *Gil Blas*), 'where people amused themselves tremendously' ('on s'est amusé prodigeusement', *L'Intransigeant* judged). Some people felt genuinely shocked by this 'extremely filthy, monstruous, savage, and violent play' ('pièce fort ordurière, monstrueuse, sauvage et violent'). Others were bored by the long lyrical tirades of the Poet/Idiot figure, as *L'Intransigeant* reported, and *Gil Blas* stated: 'This digestive allegory amused us, but then seemed a bit long. [...] The spectators got rather bored and did not fail to protest.'

Marinetti, obviously, had expected such a reception to his play, and was prepared to repeat the trick he had played on his audiences during the première of *Poupées électriques*. He was ready to present himself in front of the curtain and to fuel the fire by making a suitable announcement. But Lugné-Poë intervened and warned him that this was against the law in France.[261] Even without such ploys, the evening developed into what later became a hallmark of Futurist theatre performances: 'The spectacle took place in the hall as well as on stage', *Le Provençal de Paris* wrote. A similar description was offered by *L'Intransigeant*: 'They performed as much in the auditorium as on stage'.[262]

Because of the violent reactions at the first night, the play only received three performances, and a planned tour to Belgium and Germany was cancelled. Marinetti enjoyed the glory of being 'the most booed author of the century',[263] adding — with a view to future productions he had in mind — 'But the century is still young!' The fact that his piece was booed and whistled at meant, for Marinetti, that he had achieved a major success. As he wrote in a 'post mortem' for *L'Intransigeant*:

> Several things have been revealed to me in one week. First of all, the moving sight of a Parisian audience amused or revolted — one never knows which — to the point of delirium. I have noticed differences from Italian audiences, because I was — yes, by God, I was! — whistled, hissed, booed at in Italy, at the Teatro Alfieri in Turin, where one of my pieces was performed 'in a meeting of locomotives in rage', as one Italian critic amusingly put it. It was more blazing and less witty. Paris is above all itself when it jeers.[264]

A year later, Marinetti would make 'The Pleasure of Being Booed' a cornerstone in his theory of Futurist theatre. This new concept of audience reception was already being demonstrated in early 1909. The performances of *Poupées électriques* and *Le Roi Bombance* were organized by Marinetti in a manner that revealed his innovatory, anti-traditional concept of art as a radical negation of all conventional aesthetics and social values. This was avant-garde art conceived as insurrection; or, as Mayakovsky put it, 'A Slap in the Face of Public Taste'.

The production of *Poupées électriques* was a first attempt to translate into the context of Italian culture a concept that had first been presented to the world by Alfred Jarry in his *Ubu Roi*. Given the fact that artistic developments in Italy lagged very much behind those in other European countries, Marinetti did well to choose a play that was just a few degrees beyond what would be considered acceptable to an Italian audience. His keen judgment payed off handsomely. *Le Roi Bombance* was a far more risky undertaking. But Marinetti knew that Parisian audiences had

261 Emmanuel Aegerter and Pierre Labracherie mention this in *Au temps de Guillaume Apollinaire* (Paris, 1945), p. 234.
262 This seemed to have applied only to the first night, because *Gil Blas* reports: 'The two performances which the Œuvre gave afterwards at the Théâtre Marigny were much calmer.'
263 F. T. Marinetti, 'Les funérailles du *Roi Bombance*', *L'Intransigeant* (12 April 1909); reprinted in Marinetti, *Teatro*, vol. 2, pp. 476–77.
264 Ibid.

strong stomachs and required a heavier dose of shock tactics. Again, his judgment proved right — the newspapers mentioned his name in one breath with the 'Battle of *Hernani*' and the scandal of *Ubu Roi*.

The next stage was to introduce this radical and subversive form of avant-garde theatre into the Italian cultural world. This is where the real history of Futurist theatre begins.

BIBLIOGRAPHY

Bibliographies

Desideri, Giovannella, 'Bibliografia generale delle opere di F. T. Marinetti', in S. Lambiase & G. B. Nazzaro, *F. T. Marinetti, futurista: Inediti, pagine disperse, documenti e antologia critica* (Naples, 1977), pp. 383–402

Eruli, Brunella, 'Bibliografia delle opere di F. T. Marinetti (1898–1909)', in *Rassegna della letteratura italiana*, Ser. VII, 72 (1968), 368–88

Novelli, Novella, 'Contributo a una bibliografia della fortuna del futurismo in Francia (1909–1920)', in *La fortuna del futurismo in Francia*, ed. by P. A. Jannini (Rome, 1979), pp. 205–69

Salaris, Claudia, *Bibliografia del futurismo 1909–1944* (Rome, 1988)

Editions

Opere di F. T. Marinetti, vol. 1: *Scritti francesi*, ed. by Pasquale A. Jannini (Milan, 1983); vol. 2: *Teoria e invenzione futurista*, ed. by Luciano de Maria (Milan, 1968); vol. 3: *La grande Milano tradizionale e futurista. Una sensibilità italiana nata in Egitto*, ed. by L. de Maria (Milan, 1969)

Teatro, ed. by Giovanni Calendoli, 3 vols (Rome, 1960)

Selected Writings, ed. by R. W. Flint (London, 1972)

Stung by Salt and Water: Creative Texts of the Italian Avant-gardist F. T. Marinetti, ed. by Richard J. Pioli (New York, 1987)

La Conquête des étoiles. Poème épique (Paris, 1902, 2nd edn 1904, 3rd edn 1909); transl. *La conquista delle stelle. Poema epico* (Milan s.d. [1920])

Gabriele d'Annunzio intime (Milan s.d. [1903]), transl. *D'Annunzio intimo* (Milan s.d. [c. 1905/06])

La Momie sanglante (Milan s.d. [1904])

Destruction. Poèmes liriques (Paris, 1904); transl. *Distruzione. Poema futurista* (Milan, 1911, 2nd edn s.d. [1920])

Le Roi Bombance. Tragédie satirique en 4 actes, en prose (Paris, 1905); transl. *Re Baldoria. Tragedia satirica in 4 atti, in prosa* (Milan, 1910, 2nd edn 1920, 3rd edn 1944)

La Ville charnelle (Paris, 1908); transl. *Lussuria-Velocità* (Milan, 1921)

Les Dieux s'en vont, d'Annunzio reste (Paris, 1908)

Poupées électriques: Drame en trois actes avec une préface sur le futurisme (Paris, 1909); transl. *Elettricità sessuale* (Milan, 1920)

'L'explosion du "Roi Bombance" à Paris', in *Poesia*, 5, nos 3–6 (April–July 1909), 38–51

Mallarmé. Versi e prose. Prima traduzione italiana di F. T. Marinetti (Milan s.d. [1916])

'Autoritratto' in *Scatole d'amore in conserva* (Rome, 1927), pp. 7–28

'Alessandria d'Egitto' in *Marinetti e il Futurismo* (Rome, 1929)

Il fascino dell'Egitto (Milan, 1933)

L'Africa generatrice e ispiratrice di poesia e arti (Rome, 1940)

'Lulu', in *Theatre Three*, no. 2 (Spring 1987), 53–58

Studies on Marinetti's early writings

Agnese, Gino, *Marinetti: Una vita esplosiva* (Milan, 1990)

Altomare, Libero [i.e. Remo Mannoni], *Incontri con Marinetti e il futurismo* (Rome, 1954, 2nd edn 1986)

Andréoli-de Villers, Jean-Pierre, 'Marinetti inedito: La sua rivista egiziana', in *L'osservatore politico-letterario*, 28, no. 6 (June 1982), 94–101

Andreani, Stefano, *Marinetti e l'avanguardia della contestazione* (Rome, 1974)

Baldissone, Guisi, 'Marinetti prefuturista', in G. Baldissone, *Filippo Tommaso Marinetti* (Milan, 1986), pp. 20–53

Bellonzi, Fortunato, *F. T. Marinetti* (Pisa, 1929)

Bellonzi, Fortunato, *Saggio sulla poesia di Marinetti* (Urbino, 1943)

Bergmann, Pär, '*Modernolatria*' et '*Simultaneità*': *Recherches sur deux tendances dans l'avant-garde littéraire en Italie et en France à la veille de la première guerre mondiale* (Uppsala, 1962)

Bucci, C., 'Primi passi di Marinetti', in *Italia letteraria* (13 September 1931)

Cornell, Kenneth, *The Post-symbolist Period: French Poetic Currents, 1900–1920* (New Haven, 1958)

Décaudin, Michel, *La Crise des valeurs symbolistes* (Toulouse, 1960)

De Maria, Luciano, 'La chiave dei simboli di "Re Baldoria"', in *Il dramma*, vol. 6 (1969)

De Micheli, Mario, *La matrice ideologico-letteraria dell'eversione fascista* (Milan, 1976)

Domino, Ignazio, *F. T. Marinetti* (Palermo, 1911)

Drovetti, Giovanni, 'Marinetti e il futurismo', in *La difesa dell'arte*, 2, no. 9 (18 March 1910), 2–3

Enrile, A., 'Coincidentia oppositorum in "Destruction" di Marinetti', in *Metaphorein*, vol. 5 (1979)

Enrile, A., 'La "Conquête des Etoiles"', in *Es* (September–December 1979)

Eruli, Brunella, 'Preistoria francese del futurismo', in *Rivista di letterature moderne e comparate*, 23 (1970), 245–90

Gori, Gino, 'F. T. Marinetti', in G.Gori, *Il mantello d'Arlecchino* (Rome, 1914), pp. 193–211

Jannini, Pasquale A., 'La rivista "Poesia" di Marinetti e la letteratura francese', in *Rivista di letterature moderne e comparate*, 19 (1966), 210–19

Lambase, S. & Nazzaro, G.B., *Marinetti e i futuristi: Marinetti nei colloqui e nei ricordi dei futuristi italiani* (Milan, 1978)

Lambase, S. & Nazzaro, G.B., *F. T. Marinetti futurista: Inediti, pagine disperse, documenti e antologia critica* (Naples, 1977)

Lista, Giovanni (ed.), *Marinetti et le futurisme: Etudes, documents, iconographie* (Lausanne, 1977)

Lista, Giovanni, 'Marinetti auteur dramatique', in: G. G. Lemaire, *F. T. Marinetti: Autoportrait et les amours futuristes* (Paris, 1984), pp. 219–30

Lista, Giovanni, *La Scène futuriste* (Paris, 1989)

Livio, Gigi, *Il teatro in rivolta: Futurismo, grottesco, Pirandello e pirandellismo* (Milan, 1976)

Lorenzini, Niva, 'Antiwagneriana', in: *Alfabeta / La Quinzaine littéraire*, May 1986: Special Issue Futurismo Futurismi, pp. 21–23

Lucini, Gian Pietro, 'Meccanismi femminili?', in *La ragione* (25 October 1909), repr. in G. P. Lucini, *Marinetti, futurismo, futuristi* (Bologna, 1975), pp. 93–103

Luthi, Jean-Jacques, *Introduction à la littérature d'expression française en Egypte (1798–1945)* (Paris, 1974)

Marcadé, Jean-Claude (ed.), *Présence de F. T. Marinetti: Actes du colloques international tenu à l'UNESCO (15–17 Juin 1976)* (Lausanne, 1982)

Marcianti Tripodi, Giovanni Battista, *Il senso occulto nella 'Conquista delle Stelle' di F. T. Marinetti* (Naples, 1933)

Mariani, Gaetano, *Il primo Marinetti* (Florence, 1970)

Mariani, Gaetano, *Preistoria del futurismo: La formazione letteraria di F. T. Marinetti, 1897–1908* (Rome, 1970)

Marinelli, Donald, *Origins of Futurist Theatricality: The Early Life and Career of F. T. Marinetti* (Ph.D. Thesis, University of Pittsburgh, 1987)

Marinelli, Donald, 'Marinetti's "Lulu"', in *Theatre Three*, no. 2 (Spring 1987), 53–58

Marinetti domani: Convegno di studi nel primo centenario della nascita di FTM (Rome, 1977)

F. T. Marinetti ed il futurismo, Exh. cat. (Milan: Biblioteca Comunale, 1969)

Martin, Marianne W., 'Futurism, Unanimism and Apollinaire', in *Art Journal*, 28 (1969), 258–68

Martin, Marianne W., *Futurist Art and Theory (1909–1915)* (Oxford, 1968)

Menichi, Carlo Vanni (ed.), *Marinetti il futurista*, exh. cat. (Viareggio: Fondazione Carnevale, 1988)

Pànteo, Tullio, *Il poeta Marinetti* (Milan, 1908)

Pavolini, Corrado, *F. T. Marinetti* (Rome, 1924)

Pinottini, Marzio, 'L'unanimismo e l'estetica del futurismo', in *Unanimismo Jules Romains*, ed. by P. A. Jannini & S. Zoppi (Rome/Paris 1978), pp. 95–111

Piscopo, Ugo, 'Marinetti prefuturista: Note su alcune figure della produzione francese giovanile di F. T. Marinetti', in *Présence de F. T. Marinetti*, ed. by Jean-Claude Marcadé (Lausanne, 1982), pp. 141–55

Ragghianti, Angelo, *Marinetteide o Marionetteide?* (Rome, 1909)

Roche-Pézard, Fanette, 'Marinetti et l'anarchie', in *Présence de F. T. Marinetti*, ed. by Jean-Claude Marcadé (Lausanne, 1982), pp. 127–32

Romani, Bruno, *Dal simbolismo al futurismo* (Florence, 1969)

Saccone, Antonio, *Marinetti e il futurismo* (Naples, 1984)

Salaris, Claudia, *Filippo Tommaso Marinetti* (Florence, 1988)

Scott, Clive, *Vers Libre: The Emergence of Free Verse in France 1886–1914* (Oxford, 1990)

Sonn, Richard D., *Anarchism and Cultural Politics in Fin de Siècle France* (Lincoln, Nebraska, 1989)

Taillade, Guy, 'Unanimisme, Futurisme, Abbaye de Créteil', in *Bulletin des amis de Jules Romains*, 7, no. 23 (March 1981), 15–25

Vaccari, Walter, *Vita e tumulti di F. T. Marinetti* (Milan, 1959)

Viviani, Alberto, *Il poeta Marinetti e il futurismo* (Turin, 1940)

Wynne, M. & Barbi Marinetti, L. (eds), *F. T. Marinetti and Futurism: Catalogue of an Exhibition in the Beinecke Rare Book and Manuscript Library* (New Haven: Yale University, 1983)

Zimei, Artemisia, *Marinetti narratore sintetico dinamico di guerre e amori* (Rome, 1941)

INDEX